Chapter 1.
"It is easier for a needle to pass through the eye of a camel, than for a fish van to enter the Kingdom of Plotchka."

Thursday 18th Marz, 1000.
Usually the sight of the Prime Minister's limousine heading towards the Winter Palace was entirely uninteresting but today, the Prime Minister had the task of requesting the king to dissolve parliament so that an election could be held in six weeks' time.

The constitution provided that the minimum term for a parliament was two years and six months. It also provided that an election must be held no later than the following Saturday after three years had elapsed since the previous election.

As expected, when the Prime Minister's limousine returned to the parliament building, the flag of the Kingdom of Plotchka was ceremoniously lowered and then immediately placed into storage. The election was called for Saturday, 1st of Mai and the flag would remain in storage until the next government was decided and they once again sat.

Often the greatest ideas are conceived in jest and as the view of the lowering of the flag of Plotchka came on the television in a certain factory, one such idea was conceived.

In the town of Astari; in the province of Eoss Plotchka; in a washing machine factory; in the lunchroom, Paul Castagni and Robert Ilyanich were watching the one o'clock news on the state run Channel 5A. Channel 5A was the more serious of the two state run channels and whilst Channel 5 continued with its comedy film about a Soviet Cosmonaut who went back in time to the American Wild West, Channel 5A interrupted its agricultural news program 'The Farming File' to bring forth news of the election announcement.

Paul started booing at the television and threw a tissue at the screen in disgust. Voting was compulsory and even though it was only once every three or so years, he didn't want his morning of loafing on the couch and eating potato chips, disturbed.

Robert on the other hand, pulled out his smart phone and began looking through the Electoral Office's website. The rules said that you only needed four percent of the vote to receive an expenses allowance of six hundred thousand Lek. Since registration cost only one hundred and fifty thousand Lek, you could make four hundred and fifty thousand by doing pretty close to nothing, provided enough people voted for you and given the animosity to politicians generally, this seemed simple enough.

Robert explained his idea to Paul who immediately scoffed at the idea.

"You can't be serious, can you?"
"Well, why not?"
"What makes you think that anyone would vote for you of all people?"
"I don't."
"Then the idea is stupid."
"Yeah, but weren't you just throwing rolled up bits of paper at the television a second ago?"
"Yeah. So."
"So, if you're that angry, how many people do you think would be angry enough in a hundred thousand to say 'nuts to everyone' and then vote for someone who wasn't either that guy or the other guy?"
"You are serious."
"I wouldn't have suggested it otherwise."
"What on earth would make you do such a daft thing?"
"We choose to go to the polls and do the other things, not because they are hard, but because they are easy and we a dog lazy!"
"Hear hear!"

When the factory whistle went at one-thirty, Paul went back to his part of the factory where he fitted electronic control units and Robert went to his part of the factory where he mounted washing drums directly onto motor spindles. The idea didn't escape him though and refused to be let go. Its voice would not be silenced and when the final whistle went at five-thirty, Robert walked home and talked it over with himself in the same way that a madman talks to clouds.

Thursday 18th Marz, 1000.

Early spring evenings in Plotchka are characterised by mists that don't know if they want to be frosts and frosts that would prefer to be snow. Although Marz is the driest month of the year, the long tendrils of winter that refuse to let go can still be felt. During evenings like this, Robert's sixth storey apartment provided little respite against the cold. The building which was not built from the finest concrete that the communists had to offer, did not retain heat from the day and the central heating pipes would often freeze at night.

Robert would often be found on the couch with his wife Katherine, under a grey fleecy blanket with their two cats Columbine and Harlequin for company. Cats in particular know where the warmest places are in winter and the coolest places are in summer and so, for the period from Novambre to Avril, they were almost like permanent fixtures.

Katherine knew that something was up with Robert because instead of watching television, he was staring at the ceiling, which was something that he often did whilst lost in thought. She quizzed him about it.

"What are you thinking about?"

That single question has been the bane of many husbands the world over. It is often one of the scariest questions for a man to hear from the one he loves because it has the potential to be loaded with a whole truckload of cornucopias of innuendo and intrigue. This time though, Katherine almost felt as though she was better off not knowing the answer.

"Oh, I'm just thinking about running for parliament," said Robert.

"Yeah, right. As if that'll ever happen. You'll never be Prime Minister."

"I don't intend to be."

"Well, you'll probably never be a politician either."

"I don't intend to be that either."

"Then what's the point of running for parliament?"

"The money."

"The money?"

Katherine was confused and slightly angry. She thought he was playing a game with her, until he spoke further.

"If you happen to get at least four percent of the vote in the election, then the Electoral Office will pay you six hundred thousand Lek to cover your expenses."

"It's expensive to run for parliament."

"Not really. It only costs a hundred and fifty thousand to be registered as a candidate. If you get that four percent of the vote, you're four hundred and fifty thousand ahead."

"What about printing flyers telling people how to vote?"

"If you don't print any, it's not an expense."

"Well I still think that your idea is dumb. Where're you going to get the money from to register as a candidate?"

"You know that money I've been saving so that I can get a new car?"

"Yes?"

"I'd use some of that."

"So really, this is all one giant gamble. Look, if you want to throw a hundred and fifty thousand Lek down the toilet then that's you're problem. You'll just have to drive around in your little dodgy little Tigr a while longer."

"I know... I know."

They didn't speak about it for the rest of the evening. Robert was fully aware of the what the gamble was going to cost him but if he won, it would all be worth it. Robert's Plotchkan-built Tigr 120 was a 1.2L car built in the last throes of communism before it imploded and collapsed in on itself. The Tigr was sans all of the mod-cons that one would expect from a modern car including such optional features as FM on the radio and a heater. There were jokes about cars being built in Britain on a Friday, or that some Italian cars would rust away. All Plotchkan-built Tigrs were Friday cars and rust wasn't just a hazard of late-models, it was de rigeur.

Katherine was right though, this was a gamble. It was a gamble which if he lost, would see him continue to drive around at barely 100km/h on the motorway, for a few years longer. If the gamble paid off though, he would no longer be a chicane; no longer be a slow-moving hazard. He would be for the first time in his entire driving career, driving a car that displayed competence.

Friday 19th Marz, 1000.
Whilst the members of parliament were all hugging each other and saying their goodbyes from the current term, Robert stood in line in the Post Office with one hundred and fifty Thousand Lek notes. The One Thousand Lek note had a man with a moustache on one side who Robert had once heard about in primary school but had long since forgotten why they were famous and on the back, it had a picture of a combine harvester: presumably as a nod to the old One Thousand Lek note which also had a picture of a combine harvester, next to the sickle and star.
The lady behind the counter processed his payment without so much as a smile and she was singularly uninterested. This was a payment to a government department; the kind of thing that she processed hundreds of daily. After giving the form to her and having it stamped by someone in the back office, all Robert had to show for his registration and one hundred and fifty thousand Lek, was a pink chit and a receipt. If this was politics, it was as dull as dish water.

Monday 12th, Avril 1000.
The Globe newspaper as a newspaper of record, published all sorts of public notices. Usually they were court appearance notices for ne'er-do-wells and law breakers but at other times they were announcements of things like probate, company deregistrations and people who were declared bankrupt. Today, they had a full listing of every electorate in the country; along with every candidate and the party they were running for.
Robert was out on the factory floor, testing belt drives and checking balance weights on washing machines, in final checks before they left the factory, when his boss Neumann called him up to his office.
Robert feared the worst. The only reason anyone was called up to that little box in the sky was to be reprimanded and then hurled back down to earth again. Walking through the factory and to the base of the stairs which led to the heavens was a walk across the barren wastelands of one's own fears. Last year, an older man who was just ten days from retirement and sitting on a very large pension heard the call and collapsed in a heap, dead, before he even made it to the stairs. They were going to present him with a gold watch and a plaque for fifty-two years' service but he never made it.

As Robert walked to the end of a row of machines, he heard a slow clap begin. *Clap* *Clap* *Clap* *Clap*, went the steady beat from a hundred pairs of hands.*Clap* *Clap* *Clap* *Clap*, they continued as he walked down the central aisle between the machines; with a hundred pairs of equally scared eyes fixed upon him as though he were their sacrifice for some malevolent god who was only temporarily appeased.

As he ascended the flight of stairs, he looked up to the golden glass canopy high above him. The light it threw down the stairwell was sulphurous and gave everything a jaundiced look; his skin took on the same hue as someone who had suffered serious organ failure.

He knocked on the door of his boss, the name of whom he did not know and likewise only knew his because it only appeared on the payroll. The office like the four others up here had a horizontal slit window, which was used for looking down upon the minions below.

His boss had a high backed, tartan chair (leather or even faux-leather was deemed to extravagant up here) which faced the window. He did not bother to spin around and show his face and instead spoke with a voice which was part army captain and part steam release valve.

"Mister Ilanyich, mechaniker 46."
"Sir?"
"Reading about you, we have. Saw your name in the newspaper, we did. Pondered your possible mutiny, we did. Thought better of it and called you up here, we did."

It didn't matter whether it was a poor command of the language or a deliberate attempt to instill fear, either way it sounded creepy and made Robert's skin crawl. If his boss suddenly spun around and turned into a giant lizard, then it would not seem out of place at all.

"Mister Ilanych," slowly and quietly hissed the unseen boss, "it is good that you have not joined a political party with malicious intent. We ask you though, are you attempting some sort of uprising or industrial action. We would not take kindly to that."

"Sir, may I say something?" asked Robert.

"Yes," hissed his boss.

"I only put my name down as a candidate in the hope of getting four percent of the vote and claiming the election allowance."

"Is that all?"

"Yes sir."

"Then we have no further need to discuss anything. We are otherwise happy with your performance."

"Thank you sir."

Robert made his way back down the stairs. Each step downwards was a step further away from danger. He imagined chariots chasing after him as per the Exodus, or perhaps a giant boulder rolling down the stairs sent to crush him for his insolence but there was nothing. As he walked back across the factory floor, normality had returned and he couldn't remember ever being so happy to see a washing machine with a broken transfer gear than he was right then.

Robert spent the rest of the afternoon in a state of quiet enjoyment; quite pleased that his shape shifting lizard boss had not eaten him. If the remote chance that he did win the election came to fruition, then writing his resignation letter would be a sweet bonus prize.

Saturday 24th, Avril 1000.

A week out from the election both Prime Ministerial hopefuls were out touring the nation.

Anton Diakonos of the Konservat Demokratik Party visited a chocolate factory and a chemical processing plant which made inorganic phosphates. He praised industry leaders and tried to work the words 'get moving' into every speech that he gave. Television channels 8 & 12 who traded in sound bites were only too eager to follow the big blue campaign bus around. Anton whose wardrobe in the six months leading to the election was as drab as an album of the world's best electric motor noises, suddenly adopted a fashion sense which stretched from azure to navy and every shade of blue in between.

United Labour hopeful, Petr Brewin stuck to greys and black but made sure that he wore golden ties and handkerchiefs. He was keen to be seen in as many industrial sites as he possibly could be and on this last Saturday, he visited a General Motors factory.

The auto giant had threatened to close the engine shop, citing rising labour costs despite some of the lowest average wages in continental Europe (Plotchka was not part of the EU and had its application declined in 997) and if elected, Petr promised to fight for the good of the workers and do his best to secure their jobs.

United Labour could never govern any parliament in its own right and required the help of the Socialist Robots (so named after the Czech word for 'worker'). The Robots never expected to gain enough seats in the Federal government and didn't particularly bother with promoting their leadership. Their magazine the 'Sinister Left Monthly' had already been out since the beginning of the month and the next edition would not be out until after the election. Their manifesto was already well known among those who were likely to vote for them anyway and so they saw it as redundant to promote their cause harder.

Robert did what he always did every Saturday; he vacuumed the apartment, took the laundry down to the laundromat at the end of the street and sat in the same spot in the same cafe as he had done for five years; ordered a café americano and read the letters to the editor. Although The Globe was a reputable centre-right newspaper, it tended to push the editorial line of its owners a little too hard. This was countered by a letters section which was dominated mainly by people complaining about either the government in general or specifically about articles that they didn't like in the newspaper.
Katherine went to the local tennis club on Saturday mornings, she had tried to convince Robert to come but he had proven to be quite rubbish at the sport and preferred to do something useful. This trade worked well. She would spend her Saturday with friends and he would make up for being totally useless around the apartment for the rest of the week.

Wednesday 28th, Avril 1000.

Democracy had only arrived in Plotchka in 979 and whilst the previous year it had watched George HW Bush and Bill Clinton's debates for the U.S. presidency, the idea wasn't attractive to the leaders of a new parliamentary system. It would take until 991 before the idea was floated but it wasn't until 994 that a series of televised debates were held between the two leaders in Plotchka.

In this series of debates, Anton Diakonos was again determined to push the idea that he would help the nation 'get moving' by lowering income taxes but at the same time, he wanted to raise the VAT and this infuriated lower and middle class people. Petr Brewin, who didn't really have a strong policy barrow to push, mentioned that he would address the national wage case if elected and that his government would work with unions to try to curb inflation.

One of Plotchka's biggest problems since the fall of communism was that the country had had a stellar period of economic growth but people's incomes hadn't really risen. Economic growth had exceeded twelve percent per annum, every year for more than a decade and in that time period, GDP had more than trebled but people's pay packets were still roughly the same size they were in real terms in 990. There were now 117 Lek to the US Dollar and imported goods were becoming even more expensive.

The European Union was still very cagey about dealing with the Banca Plotchki and although the Plotchki Government had passed many pieces of key legislation, The European Central Bank still saw Plotchka as a serious sovereign risk and was worried about it needing to be bailed out at a later date.

Anton Diakonos said that any government that he would lead, would strive for greater ties and integration towards formulating a proper European policy but Petr Brewin who having seen how the old Plotchki Central Executive Committee had dealt with the six provinces, didn't want a central European legislature doing likewise.

While the debate was going on, viewers on Channel 5A who had downloaded an app could collectively decide who was winning the debate at any given point. Robert watched the debate intensely because he liked the spectacle of it all but Katherine sat on the couch knitting a new blanket because Harlequin had chewed through the last one.

"Who do you think will win this debate?"
"Huh?"
"The leaders' debate, who do you think will win it?"
"Oh I don't care."
"What about the 'worm' that shows what the public thinks?"
"Oh that. Is 'hanging itself with its own body' an option?"
"No."
"Then I don't care about that either."

Katherine didn't have to wait for long. Come midnight, there would be an official media blackout; during which time no radio, television or print advertisements would be allowed. Technically the law also applied to the internet but trying to police that was like trying to smell the colour 'nine'.

Monday 28th Marz, 1000.
Every day Robert had checked the mailbox down stairs and every day, he was disappointed. Every day which passed without a confirmation that he would be on the ballot paper was a day which was wasted as far as he was concerned. Like a small boy waiting for a present which never came, he grew less and less hopeful of seeing anything but on the ninth day of waiting, there was a small green envelope from the Electoral Office.

Without even taking it up stairs, he slid his finger under the flap and ran it down a fold. The only contents in the envelope were a one-page letter thanking him for his candidacy, a receipt for one hundred and fifty thousand Lek from the Electoral Office and a sky blue piece of paper which was four inches wide and five inches long.

It bore the seal of the Kingdom of Plotchka on the top left hand corner, a circle on the top right (for the electoral officers to mark, once it had been counted) and the words:

"BALLOT PAPER
COMMUNE ASSEMBLY
EOSS PLOTCHKA
ELECTORAL DIVISION OF ASTARI"

Robert read on. His excitement was palpable.

"Number the Boxes from 1 to 4 in the order of your choice.
☐ IND Robert Ilanyich
☐ ULP Dom Freyr
☐ SR Cristop Kirkov
☐ KDP Amir Kahn
Please number every box to make your vote count.

SAMPLE - SAMPLE - SAMPLE - SAMPLE"

He could not believe it. There was his name on an official ballot paper. He Robert Ilanyich, was a listed candidate for the Division of Astari. His name would in just a few short weeks, appear in national newspapers and even if he didn't win, it did not matter. If 3900 people put a one in the box next to his name, even if they were just doing it because they really couldn't care and put in a donkey vote through sheer apathy and ignorance, he would quadruple his money.

He ran upstairs to tell Katherine who was unimpressed and wanted to go back to watching a game show where people guessed amounts of money which were printed on cards inside of suitcases. Nobody really understood the game or why it even existed but Robert saw the irony that whilst the majority of people were quite happy to watch people open suitcases which didn't affect their lives, they didn't want to watch or understand how to properly fill in a ballot paper which would affect their lives.

Friday, 30th Avril, 1000.
The day before the election, Robert was again called up into the office in the sky. Instead of an unseen and faceless voice to greet him, he saw a small officious man in a grey suit who had the equally grey personality of a block of concrete. The voice was the same as before but instead of being dismembered and unattached, it was slightly more human; or as close Atlas it could get to being human without actually getting there.

"Mister Ilanyich, do take a seat. Do."
Robert sat.
"It is not that we object to you running for parliament, it's that we are worried about a worker led rebellion which would lead to strikes and industrial action. This factory has been running quite efficiently for twenty-one years without state control and keeping it running is something we wish. Worried about imports undercutting us on price, we are; for we know that they can make an identical product in China or Peru for less than thirty percent of our total costs."

This was very much an act of self-preservation on the boss' part, Robert thought. If he could quietly quell the man's fears, then all of this would come to an end.

"Sir? Can you please check my personnel file? If you look in there I think that you'll fund that I have never ever gone on strike and have had less than half a dozen days of sick leave in all the time I've been employed here. If I was organising some sort of workers' revolt, don't you think that I would have already done it by now?
Besides, if I was a socialist, wouldn't I have joined the Socialist Robots? If I was a labour unionist, shouldn't I have joined the United Labour Party? If I was a capitalist or a right leaning conservative, wouldn't I have joined the KDP?"
"You might be an anarchist," said the boss.
"If I was an anarchist, I probably would have smashed up machines by now. What sort of anarchist decides to run for parliament if they don't believe in the system?"
"That's true."
"I'm running as an independent so that I can pick up just four percent of the vote and claim the election allowance. The only '-ist' I am is an opportunist."

The boss closed his and murmured slightly. He waved hand and in the direction of the door.

"I shall see you on Monday, Mister Ilanyich. Please close the door on your way out."

Robert closed the door quietly has he left. He stepped back into the stairwell and made the long walk back down to the factory floor. Thus time though, the golden light which came from above, was not the stain of jaundice but the helpful shade of a canary; which indicated that he was still alive.

Saturday, 1st Mai, 1000.
Finally the day of the election came and instead of a lot of opinion polls which did not matter, everywhere around the country, people were standing in queues; lining up for the only poll which did matter.

"The Election of The Millennium" was the strapline that The Globe had been running for the six weeks of the campaign and although the very first election after the fall of the communists was probably more important, the media was still keen to extract as much publicity and interest as they could, for that sold newspapers.
Day after day, the Globe had showed pictures of the Prime Minister Anton Diakonos visiting factories, visiting construction sites and anywhere else that gave him an excuse to wear a hard hat, strap on a high-visibility jacket and stand next to either big industrial machinery or posing with tools as though he was doing hard physical labour, when in actual fact, his previous job before becoming a politician was as a barrister and he barely knew one end of a shovel from the other.
The Star threw its weight behind the Leader of the Opposition Petr Brewin and tried to frame the election campaign as a boxing match. For almost the entire campaign, it placed a graphic of a boxing glove in one corner and a bell in the other of the masthead.

There was something of a disconnect in message though because it tried to depict Brewin as something of a fatherly figure; showing him with school children, attending child care centres, hospitals and doing mundane sorts of things like taking public transport.

The Prime Minister Anton Diakonos and the Leader of the Opposition Petr Brewin, had both run surprisingly similar campaigns; both arguing that theirs was the best party to lead the country into the new millennium, which was totally bizarre because the rest of the world had celebrated its own millennium celebrations more than a decade and a half ago. Plotchka was a stubborn kingdom and old habits such as its unique date system were resistant to change.

Diakonos was arguing that his Konservat Demokratik Party government was best poised to navigate through the waters of uncertainty as it had experience but Petr Brewin called for a change of government; arguing that the ruling party was growing long in the tooth and that the country needed a more vibrant leader. Brewin's United Labour Party had made it part of its manifesto that if elected, it would try and push for membership to the European Union and acceptance back into the real world.

The largely negative campaigns from three years ago did not sit well with the public and opinion polls showed that both Diakonos and Brewin had both fallen to the lowest public approval ratings of a Prime Minister and Opposition Leader since the arrival of democracy. Both of them were keen to show that they understood the concerns and worries of the nation and both of them, aged in their mid-50s, and were also keen to be portrayed in the best possible light. As a result, their approval ratings had both climbed immensely.

Multi-Party elections in Plotchka were relatively new in the history of the nation - virtually all of the people running for office had been members of the Communist Party before it opened up the floor of parliament to other voices and had all left like rats jumping off a sinking ship.

Even in less than a generation though, the Commune Assembly which was the lower house, had already coagulated into two broad factions with the Konservat Demokrats on one side and United Labour and the Socialist Robots on the other.

The Senate was a completely different affair with each of the six provinces sending Senators elected by proportional representation. Parliament was often likened to a giant Sturm-Cake with a layer of two shades on brown at the bottom and a layer of fruits and nuts above. King Josep V who was the first monarch after the restoration was the cherry on the very top.

Diakonos' government had consistently gained approval ratings above 50% and so in the early stages of the campaign it seemed something of a fait accompli that they should be returned to power but as time wore on, the polls showed a distinct narrowing. The Globe's final poll before the election; before the media blackout, which started Thursday, showed that the KDP would gain 46% of the popular vote, with the ULP also standing at 39%. There was also a group in parliament who would probably side with the ULP called the Socialist Robot Party, which represented factory workers and they would most likely pick up 7% of the popular vote.

When Saturday morning rolled around, Prime Minister Anton Diakonos was one of the very first people to arrive at his local polling station; hoping to get his name said on the radio and television as often as possible. Petr Brewin spent the morning in a café; showing a relaxed attitude to the cameras and microphones which followed him about during the day.

The majority of Plotchkans, who still thought that elections were something of an event, went to their polling stations throughout the day, accompanied by the smells of roasting meats and the sweet smells of candy. Many polling places were set up at schools and town halls and so local groups such as citizen's associations and sporting clubs, also held fetes and stalls on election day; some even had jumping castles, clowns and face painting for the children.

Voting was compulsory under the communists and no-one had thought to change the law. There were some groups who argued that there should be voluntary voting, on the basis that people had a democratic right not to vote but the experience of other nations which did have voluntary voting, convinced most leaders that there would be unnecessary expense in trying to encourage people to come to the polls once every three years. It was just cheaper and less of a hassle to leave the law as was; apathy and pragmatism won the day.

By mid-afternoon, the long lines that had formed in the morning had dissipated and people went off to do their shopping, or watch sporting events. The people having done their duty, returned to their normal Saturday. They would tune in later that evening as results began to come in, from all over the nation. Because the election was conducted on paper ballots, they were still counted by hand and even though the polls closed at 6pm, the results would be known by about 10pm. The Senate though, would not even begin to be counted until Monday but that was all right because the Senate had fixed terms and so the current Senators would remain until Januar 1001.

At six o'clock, the polls closed and locked boxes all over the country were simultaneously opened. The television stations who had nothing to report about the election in their regular nightly bulletins, all ran with lead stories showing happy people putting their ballot papers into the locked boxes. Channels 8, 9 and 12 all had panels of official looking political pundits all trying to give their opinions on who would win the election but the two state television stations, 5 and 5A treated this Saturday like any other. Channel 5 was playing a comedy series and 5A ran with "Match Of The Day".

If you had been watching either Channel 8, 9 or 12 that evening, you would have seen an ever increasing sense of tension across the faces of the political pundits and commentators as it was becoming ever more apparent that this election was heading for a knife edge result. Seats would be declared for the KDP and then for the ULP or the SR. Some figures such as Igor Davikov who had been the Father Of The House before the election, suddenly found that they were without a seat altogether and still other up and coming go-getters had won seats which they had not expected to.

63 seats were needed to form a majority and therefore to form government and although a tumble of seats were suddenly declared between 09:30pm and 10:00pm, the two groups had both reached 50 and were nervously inching forward. Even the computers employed by the television stations which had previously predicted seats for one side or the other, had become strangely indecisive; posting messages that the results of some seats were now too close to call.

Neither Anton Diakonos nor Petr Brewin were willing to concede defeat, for they know that even if they did, the will of the people is what determines the outcome of elections. The people already had spoken, it was just becoming more difficult to determine what they had said.

As the night wore on, it suddenly dawned on many people that the result might not be known that evening; so the expected parties which were planned once the government had been declared were put on hold. Acceptance and Concession speeches which had been written, would for the moment, remain unspoken.

Of the 125 seats in the Commune Assembly, by 11pm when counting had officially stopped, there were still more than 20 undeclared seats. Many of these would go to second preferences and a few to third preferences; there was even one seat, the District of Hasemer, which would eventually be fought out on fourth preferences.

The three commercial television stations (8, 9 and 12) had more or less returned to regular programming once it had been determined that no result would immediately be forthcoming but the two state-run television stations though, took a slightly different tack. Channel 5 played the late movie as was normally scheduled but Channel 5A would continue beyond its usual 11pm news bulletin and its normal close at 11:30 and witter on with political analysis until 12:30 before it too played the nightly fanfare and went to bed.

By the time that the nation rubbed its bleary eyes upon an unknown morning, they were still not really much better off. There were still 8 unclaimed seats in the Commune and neither the Prime Minister of His Majesty's Government, Anton Diakonos; nor his counterpart, the leader of the Loyal Opposition, Petr Brewin, were prepared to concede defeat and neither could they claim victory. Without a clear idea of the makeup of the next parliament, the very idea of forming government was still impossible and without a seer into the future, the destiny of the nation was still very much up in the air - who knew how it would fall?

Sunday, 2nd Mai, 1000.
Harlequin and Columbine were impatient and began scratching their servant's door. It is an almost universally accepted fact that cats do not have masters, they have staff. Harlequin and Columbine's staff stirred in their bed as the first few rays of sunshine began to invade their apartment.

Katherine made noises that Robert should go and feed Harlequin and Columbine and he, being closest to the bedroom door, reluctantly acquiesced. It is also an almost universally accepted fact that the side of the bed that newlyweds pick on their first night together, is the side of the bed that they will sleep on, for the rest of their lives. Robert Ilanyich, was amazed at how an arbitrary decision made in Paris more than a decade ago, had lasting effects on a perfectly cosy Mai morning. He got out of bed, put on a shirt and a pair of shorts and stumbled through the apartment.

"Cat food, what is it?" he wondered. Cat food smelled like that strange meat that you were given in the army when out on patrol detail; even out there, it still wasn't easy to work out what it was made from. Dry cat food was some sort of kibble; perhaps like the sort of thing that he imagined that cosmonauts ate but cats were never going to go into space.

Robert looked into the fridge to see how much milk was left. Usually if there was something hidden in the fridge, it would be hiding behind the milk. There was no milk. Could milk hide behind itself? Barring a bout with existential set theory and the state of being or non-being, Robert decided that the best thing to do would be to go down to the corner store and buy some more milk.

He showered, shaved; dragged a razor blade across his face and stared into the bloodshot eyes staring back at him from the mirror. Like everyone else in the country, he had stayed awake long into the night, waiting for the results of the election to be announced but unlike everyone else, he was not waiting for the result of who would be the next Prime Minister.

When the election was first called, Robert had had the crazy idea that provided a candidate won just 4% of the votes in a seat, they were eligible to receive 500,000 Lek from the Electoral Commission. Since registering as a candidate cost 200,000 Lek, then he'd still be 300,000 Lek ahead. He had printed off a few flyers and "how to vote" leaflets which he handed out to people in the queue to vote at polling stations yesterday but that was pretty well much all the work that he had done.

With just under 98,000 voters in the electorate, he needed less than 4000 of them to put a "1" in the box next to his name and since there were only four candidates in the election, he thought that running as an independent might be a way to make some easy money. Katherine thought that he was quite quite mad and that this was all a pipe dream that would end with nothing more than a couple of hundred thousand Lek being frittered away. Still, Robert dared to dream.

Robert walked down the street and bought some milk, the morning's newspaper and a packet of current buns. Even on the way back to the apartment, the air was already growing muggy with that heavy humid fug that the region was known for. Robert climbed the concrete stairs of his apartment block and heard the strains of mass, blaring from the television of the old lady who lived a few floors below. He turned the key and opened his door to see that Columbine was on the other side; waiting for him to arrive with the milk. Harlequin was dozing on the couch in the living room and only barely regarded Robert as he went into the kitchen.

Robert fussed about for a bit, made a cup of tea and toasted a currant bun before sitting out on the balcony, the one place in the whole apartment where Harlequin and Columbine did not have domain. He opened the newspaper and ignored the whole front half, instead turning to the sports section to read rumours about the Royal Cup Football Final which was going to be played later that afternoon. His team, St Iames Dinamo had somehow scrapped its way past opponents far more celebrated than itself and had booked its place to meet FC Shapelle in the chase for silverware.

Robert was engrossed in reading about anticipated tactics and formations when Katherine started banging on the glass door of the balcony, ludicrously excited; her hair still wet from her morning shower.

"What is it?"

"This is… that is… I don't even know where to begin…"

"What?"

"You're the new Member for Astari."

"What?"

"The Member for Astari has the floor."

"I… I…"

"You're not going to make a very good politician if you just stand there like a freshly caught fish."

Robert opened his mouth but the words did not come. What words were there?

Katherine began phoning everyone that they knew and Robert stood in the middle of the living room in stunned confusion. By running to be a member of parliament, not even he had honestly expected to win and even he would be the first to admit that it had all been an exercise in cynicism and foolishness.

"Wait. What? What's going on? How did you find out that I'd been elected?"

"A man from the Electrical Commission rang up and said that you had."

"Did he leave a number?"

"Oh yes. I wrote it down."

Robert telephoned the Electoral Commission, still shocked that his impossible gamble; which not even he believed would work, had paid off. Katherine listened on as Robert's conversation with a public servant ran staccato for three minutes. Robert's brain simply refused to comprehend what was going on. He walked back to the balcony and picked up the newspaper; then turned to the front half which he had neglected to read before.

Electorate of Astari:
KDP Amir Kahn* – 32,286 (32.81%)
IND Robert Ilanyich – 30,779 (31.27%)
ULP Dom Freyr – 24,818 (25.21%)
SR Cristop Kirkov – 10,501 (10.67)
*incumbent
Electorate decided on preferences.

Robert could not believe it. For just appearing on a ballot paper as an independent, the electorate must have decided that he was worth their second preference; even without a formal campaign. It has been said that oppositions don't generally win elections; governments lose them, and in this case, if a bowl of borscht had been put up as a candidate, it would have been returned as the new Member for Astari.
Robert had been elected to parliament, not for having a good platform of policies, not for being a skilled orator, not because he had charm or candour but simply because he was not one of the other guys.
He didn't know whether to be proud, or ashamed, or happy, or anything. As Katherine continued to telephone people, he slumped on the couch as the thought that his life would inexorably change, hit him like a Kamaz meeting a rockmelon. Winning an election was one thing but they would either have to move or he would face a very long daily commute. He decided that disturbing Katherine with this thought right away would be unfair and so he continued to sit with it as it began to needle away at his mind.

When nightfall came, their little apartment held more people than it ever had before. Robert and Katherine had never held a party like this and now there were people from both inside the building as well as their friends and family.

"Come on, Robert. The people are waiting for you to say something."

Although surrounded by friends and family, Robert felt a strange sort of guilt. In every achievement in Robert's life there was a common thread in all of them – achievement. In every other endeavour, he had worked quite hard to reach a goal but with this, he'd done hardly anything for his reward. Robert didn't really feel like he could accept congratulations for what amounted to in his mind, a case of dumb luck. Nevertheless, the small crowd of people stood in silence; hanging on the words which were to come out of his mouth.
He spoke, slowly at first but a sense of occasion got to him and almost visibly, he grew a spine; as if he actually grew taller.

"To those of us here, my family, my friends, those people who live in the building who wanted to show up at a party, I'd like to thank you all for being here. To the more than thirty thousand people of the Electorate of Astari most of whom I've never met, I'd also like to thank you and hope to vindicate the trust that you've placed in me.
There are people who have worked hard and long at the game of politics and I am not one of those people. Maybe it is the will of God, maybe it is fate; maybe it is the roll of an eternal and unseen dice roll that has placed me in this position but here am I. Through reasons I cannot understand, I have been appointed your representative to the mad house in Vayav and I promise that I will take my place within its chambers and give the people of Astari their proper voice. Maybe I am yelling into a wall of sound but as from this day of Mai in the year one thousand, the people of Astari will be heard."

Cheers went up inside the room and even people on the street noticed that from that particular apartment on the sixth floor, that there was a different sort of sound in the air. Already, before the new parliament had even sat, "The Election of The Millennium" had thrown up an unexpected result. This parliament would be different.

Chapter 2.
"The north wind brings unexpected rain and gossipy tongues provoke horrified looks."

Monday, 3rd Mai, 1000.
The 6am news on Radio 1 could not repeat anything new about the election, as counting was still occurring in four electorates and it was still entirely possible for either side to win government. In theory the new Prime Minister would be known later that morning but in practice, who honestly knew how it would play out?

Robert grew bored with speculation after speculation on Radio 1 and switched to Radio 2 hoping for something better but failed. Radio 2 was playing tired music for a tired generation and so he switched to Radio 7 which was playing funky music for a funky generation; he decided that he was too old for Radio 7 but not nearly old enough for Radio 2.

Somewhere in the car (which was one of the finest examples of communist engineering; in that it was both over engineered whilst at the same time unreliable) smelled as though there was something hiding somewhere which was both old and funky. The offending smell was vaguely that of apple from a long time ago, though the signal that it was issuing was that it was probably no longer an apple but a small ecosystem. He continued to fiddle with the radio.

Back to Radio 1… Nope. Preset 1?.. Nope. Search Up… Nothing.

AM cycled upwards; counting in nine kilocycle jumps as it went but found nothing. FM also cycled upwards and also found nothing. DAB+ scanned and then beeped and continued to spit out the message "Station Not Found" before it too gave up and then AM showed its face again.

In the rear view mirror, the sun weakly shone across grey hills. Robert wished on the breeze that he could one day see the sun rise out of the ocean for set into it but Plotchka was entirely landlocked. The nearest analogue was the sun rising out of the Black Sea but he didn't know if that counted or not.

Plotchka being landlocked country had no need of a navy but for some bizarre reason, possibly to do with its failed attempt to enter NATO, had a helicopter carrier permanently stationed in Greece.

This early in the morning, the road was still subject to frost and black ice; even in Mai. Traffic though didn't seem to care much and some drivers thought that the 150km/h speed limit was more of a serving suggestion than the law; the police didn't enforce it very much either. Some cars like Robert's tried their best to even hit three digits.

Meanwhile, low slung Italian sports cars and German luxo-barges regularly whizzed past at more than 200 and all that could be seen and heard of them was a pair of red tail lights fading into the mist and sounds akin to Vivaldi's Four Seasons as played on the symphonic strains of chainsaws.

The M3 was an ugly ugly road. Motorways the world over aren't generally known for their looks and beauty but the M3 combined ugliness with a unique blend of boredom and crumbling propaganda that can only be found in formerly communist countries. Motorways in the west usually combine boredom with the occasional billboard from products enticing motorists to buy food and drink; thus requiring them to make secondary stops at the next motorway services to relive themselves and thus walk around, hopefully to purchase still more stuff.

Once you left the forest of brutalist concrete apartment complexes of the city, the M3 headed out into fields and so-called "villages" which just meant single brutalist concrete apartment complexes standing on their own. Just after you'd left the outskirts of Ovidia, there was a colossal rusted iron statue of Comrade Gregor, the founder of the nation.

Was this his vision of a workers' paradise? Most of the old buildings from the 700s and 800s had long since rotted away and now the grey and dour concrete buildings from the 900s were also on their way out, as though refusing to enter the millennium without argument.

As Robert drove on and with no radio stations to break the silence, Robert thought about his resignation letter which he would have to send to his ex-employers at the washing machine factory where he had worked even just this Friday past, now that he had unexpectedly become a member of parliament.

He was amused that the letter which he would send to them, would appear on parliamentary letterhead and that the closing line would be "Robert Ilanyich, MCA". At least, he assumed that he could use official parliamentary letterhead for that sort of thing. That was something to ask about later.

After almost two and a half hours, the final part of the journey began in earnest. The M3 began to rise quite steeply for the last 20km stretch. His little Tigr 120 began to wheeze as even as Ukrainian-built ZAZs, Russian-built ZAZs and even a Czech-built Tatra overtook him. The Plotchkan-built Tigr was such an incompetent machine that in wet weather, you had to decide whether you wanted to use either the windscreen wipers or the lights; if you dared to even think about using the indicators to make a turn, you had to submit forms in triplicate to the Transitburo at least several weeks in advance.

From 98km/h indicated with his foot flat to the floor in top gear, only a few kilometres ago, the car now sludged to 47km/h uphill. If he was going to do this journey on a regular basis, he would need a far better car; maybe something German.

After what was a herculean struggle, Robert's plucky little Tigr finally began to reach the skyline. The radio crackled back into life and Radio 1 was now discussing developments in the Middle East.

After rounding a corner which passed around a craggy monolith, he beheld a sight which he had only seen once before as a child on a school field trip; except now it was far grander.

There it was, the city of Vayav in all its planned glory; laid out like a map on a table. Vayav lay in a valley at the top of a mountain and proved that a city on top of a hill can actually be hidden provided you wrap it in red tape.

Its six main boulevards radiated out like spokes of a cartwheel and at the centre, at the very hub, sat the parliament building with its two halves in red and white brick.

Niuw General Platz as it was officially called or "The Shortcake" as it was colloquially named by everyone, was a marvel of early 900s architecture which strangely, hadn't been demolished when the communists took over in 917. By "marvel" it meant that you had to marvel at why such a hideous thing had even been allowed to stand in the first place.

The red half of The Shortcake which the Commune Assembly sat in featured twenty-two onion domes; whilst the white half of the Senate, was a strange sort of pyramid, also with an onion dome at the apex. Finer cities like Paris and London had had a dalliance with Art Deco but Vayav obviously hadn't got the message and The Shortcake was more of an experimental piece, which had worked so well that no-one repeated the experiment ever again.

The nice thing about Vayav was that the main six motorways, connected straight onto the spokes of the cartwheel. Robert didn't even need to open a map to know where to go. As he drove down one of the wide boulevards towards The Shortcake, the odd person here and there waved at him; not because he was famous or anything but because his little Tigr looked like an antique set against the backdrop of the city.

He followed to signs all the way down to the outer perimeter wall of the shortcake and remembered that he didn't need to drive to the public car parks but could use the car parks set aside for members of parliament and government staff.

He arrived at an entrance and after an explanation and waited half hour at an underground security checkpoint. The security staff had already been issued with a list of the new members of parliament and after they were satisfied that Robert was who he was supposed to be (and after demanding to see his driver's licence and passport) he was issued with a car park pass and even found a designated parking spot. Some features of bureaucracy appeared to work like a well-greased machine, even if they were inconvenient.

Inside the parliament building itself, there were more levels of security checking and staff in oversized uniforms with polished brass buttons, muttered quietly to each other before issuing Robert with an electronic swipe card and a GPS lapel pin so that they could track his whereabouts in the parliament complex.

They assigned him an office and a set of keys but when he got there, although he could turn the keys in the lock, the door still would not open. He went back to the security desk who apologised profusely and they explained that it would probably be about an hour before his office would be ready, as cleaning staff needed to go through and destroy anything that might have been left behind from its previous occupant, for security and confidentiality reasons.

Instead of being annoyed at this, Robert was quietly pleased that even the cleaning staff took their jobs so seriously. With not much else to do for the hour, he left the secure section of the building and decided to go for a wander through the public galleries, bookshops and newsstands.

Monday, 3rd Mai, 1000.

Robert's wanderings didn't last long. After about fifteen minutes, he grew bored and he found himself in the café of the public foyer. He found cold comfort with a slice of bland coffee cake and something which was billed as coffee but didn't equally didn't taste of anything either.

The security team had issued him with a mobile telephone should any news come to hand but it remained silent.

The Globe newspaper had a welcoming front page splash of Anton Diakonos and Petr Brewin with photo shopped boxing gloves squaring off against each other as though the election fight was still on in earnest, though in reality, the election had taken place and they both were in as much of a state of limbo as anyone else.

The back page of the Globe reported that Robert's football team, St Iames Dinamo, had beaten FC Shapelle 1-0 in extra time through a Marcus Rikard strike to send them through to the Royal Cup Final. Robert had missed the cup final because he'd been out on the hustings on Saturday and didn't have tickets anyway; on Sunday, he'd spent a great deal of the day asleep; exhausted.

He'd also picked up a copy of the constitution from the parliamentary bookstore for 500 Lek. It would probably woefully inadequate for the job which he would undertake for at least the next two years but it would make light reading for at least the next half hour.

Looking about the foyer, he noted that the parliament building, the Niuw General Platz, was vastly different to the brick shell which the world saw. Inside it was stark, recto-linear and cold. Every surface was either in off-form concrete and others had hard equally stark faces. It was as though you could go skating on the walls if you so desired; provided that the law of gravity could be revoked or repealed; which no doubt the radical libertarians probably would have tried, if they could get away with it.

A black square fountain, like a cube, surrounded by a metal cake tray sort of affair, stood in the middle of the foyer which was supposed to symbolise democracy springing forth from the former rigidity of the old communist state, or so the plaque read. Robert thought that all that it successfully symbolised was bad taste and a complete lack of appreciation for beauty. It was fitting that school children would place their hands in the cool water which ran down the sides of the cube and try to wet each other, for at least someone was having fun with it.
The old General Platz was a small wooden building which had dated from the 600s and had wooden crossbeams in the ceiling which would have been contemporary with an English parliament building which almost was blown to pieces, after conspirators devised a plot to pack the basement with gunpowder. Robert pondered that the Niuw General Platz should have been blown up before it was completed.
After the fall of the communists in 979, the whole process of government was opened to multi-party elections. To appease the older communist members of the legislature, the number of sitting members was opened to one hundred and twenty-five, whilst the Senate remained at sixty-two, being ten from each of the six provinces and two from the Federal Distrikta.

The communists duly split into two factions and aligned themselves along class lines. Those members with business connections joined the Konservat Demokratik Party or KDP and those who came from the old workers' collectives which were now trade unions, formed the United Labour Party. In the Senate though, the ULP further fragmented into those who had come from factories and they took on a name which had existed from even before when the communists had taken over. They took on the older Plotchki meaning of the word and decided to call themselves the Socialist Robot Party. Since this election had been out of phase with the Senate, the next Senate election wouldn't be declared until at least Aout of 1001. The KDP had 25 members in the Senate, ULP and the Robots together had 23 and there were 6 Greens and 8 independents.

The curious thing about the Plotchkan Senate was that although the lower house, the Commune Assembly, was made up of single-member constituencies and voted in by preferential voting, the Senate was a proportional representative system with the members being elected by the whole province at once. In the Commune Assembly, politics had very quickly come to be dominated by two-parties but the Senate, was like a weird mish-mash of ideologies. In five of the six Senate elections since the end of communism, there were always at least two independents or micro-parties. In the 1995 Senate election for instance, a member was elected from a party called the "Ride The Bus Party", in which the only sitting member thought that best way to hear the voice of the people was literally to ride the buses and talk to people directly. It sounded like a brilliant idea except that the member in question wasn't particularly well liked and after five months of having abuse heaped on him, he ceased to ride the bus any more.

Robert leafed through his newly acquired copy of the Constitution. Most of it defined the rules by which new provinces could be admitted and the methods by which legislation was to be voted upon. Other countries' constitutions included grand statements to do with the rights of the people but the only concession written here was that the Constitution of Plotchka provided for the "well-being and common good" of the nation, whatever that meant.

For 500 Lek, this handy little guide seemed like a good investment, however boring it turned out to be. Robert thought that it was fitting that members of parliament should know the rules which governed how they were to do their job and then he wondered if he hadn't just wasted 500 Lek because he would be issued with a copy anyway.

His government issued mobile phone rang and he walked back through the foyer and the secure area of the building to the office which would be his for the term of this parliament, which was more than likely to be no shorter than three years.

There were three rooms in his office. The first which faced the corridor contained a heavy set desk with a pine green inlay on the top. A green bankers' lamp sat on one side and a telephone sat on the other – a telephone?

Plotchka was one of those strange countries which had sat on the dismal side of the Iron Curtain and most of the general public had never owned their own landline telephones. The vast majority of Plotchki had gone from owning no telephone at all, straight to mobile telephony. Likewise, the new phenomenon of the internet had been an equally vast jump from nothing at all to fibre-optic cable internet for most people.

The central room of Robert's office contained a couch, which could be converted into a bed, a flat screen television, a small fridge and a small closet. Robert wondered if this was an ominous omen. Would he as part of his work, spend so many late nights in the office that he would need to use the bed? He hoped not.

The third and final room in the office was an almost mirror copy of the one which faced the outer corridor. It too had a door which led to an inner corridor and this made immediate sense to him. The outer corridor could be accessed by people with press passes but the inner corridor could only be accessed by people with parliamentary members' passes. This meant that whoever had designed the building oh so long ago, had thought it necessary that the business of government should be done without impedance from a prying press. Members of parliament were free to leave via the inner corridor and meet with each other without fear of annoyance. Robert also very quickly realised that all of the inner corridors had an inner glass wall around a central courtyard. It would be easy, provided you were looking, to see who was coming and going and from which offices. Probably deliberately, Robert had been issued with an office, dead bang in the centre of a run of them; so as an independent, he would be certain that sharp eyed members from the major parties, would probably tell who came in and out of his office. Already, this looked portentous.

Worse still was the visible state of four surveillance cameras, one in each of the top corners, in all three rooms. With no windows to any of the rooms, it would have been very easy for something untoward to occur within those offices; so during the 960s, in the last throes of the communist state, it was made obvious that politicians were being watched.

Robert closed the door to the inner corridor; left the door to the outer corridor open and then closed the door to the central room behind him.

He wasn't exactly sure at this point what he was supposed to do. There was no correspondence for him to answer and there were no documents for him to look at. He wondered if he would be given notices of impending legislation which was to be voted on but seeing as there was no government formed as yet, there probably wouldn't be any for a while.

He switched on the television but found that the only four channels available to him were a closed circuit view of both the Commune Assembly and the Senate, and the two state television stations, 5 and 5A. Channel 5 was running educational programs for primary schools and Channel 5A ran with its usual morning news coverage. By now there were one hundred and nineteen seats declared in the election race with the Konservat Demokratik Party winning 59, the United Labour Party had won 50 and the Socialist Robots had won 8. He had won a seat and there was one other independent. Six seats remained outstanding and with a majority of sixty-three required to form government, even now it was still possible for either side to win.

A parliamentary official arrived with a laptop and a tablet, which Robert duly signed for and another official followed not long after with forms to fill out so that things like wages and taxation were properly dealt with. 5A News reported that counting had ceased in the Electorate of Nord-Marx and that another independent had been declared as the winner.
By this time, the sun began to shine down into the central courtyard and after reading the emails which came on the internal email system, Robert locked both the outer and inner doors to his office and headed downstairs to a cafeteria provided for the use of members of parliament and staff.
Nobody regarded him as he handed over more than a thousand Lek for a sandwich and a drink and there were groans and a sense of disappointment could be heard from a group of men in suits over in one corner as three more seats were declared bringing the number of independents to three and the United Labour Party to fifty-two seats - three seats remained.

Robert went back to his office and again read through the terms of his employment contract as a member of parliament. He couldn't believe his eyes when he read that he was entitled to a motor allowance of one and a half million Lek. One and a half million? Were they insane?
Of course, he very soon realised that they more or less expected parliamentarians to use it because simply travelling to and from his home would put a lot of wear on peoples' motor cars.

Robert phoned Katherine who was initially delighted and then rather saddened as it dawned on her that Robert needed a new car to get to and from work and that she would be left with the Tigr. Robert did a brief search on the internet and found that there were plenty of second hand motor cars which could be had for three-quarters of a million Lek and that in they traded in the Tigr, with his motor allowance they could buy two cars quite easily. Katherine acquiesced and practically demanded that he trade in the Tigr immediately so that they knew how much would be left for her car.

As there was going to be no parliament sitting for the afternoon, Robert decided to leave early and he traded in the Tigr for a small German hatchback; leaving eight-hundred fifty thousand Lek for Katherine to buy her new car. Robert was hardly sorry to see the Tigr go and his newish metallic blue hatchback even had a bolt of lightning on the badge – this was a good sign.

The journey back down the M3 was totally unlike the one which he had made in the morning. Instead of being passed by trucks and buses, his new blue hatchback easily did 150 on the motorway; Robert decided to name his new blue companion "Bolt". Bolt didn't even have the problem that the Tigr did, in that Radio 1 came in crisp and clean (even on DAB+) for the entire trip home.

By the end of the trip home, the last of the seats had been declared and the Konservat Demokratik Party now sat on sixty, the United Labour Party remained on fifty-two seats, the Socialist Robot Party also remained on eight, but there were now five independents. This mean that there were sixty on one side and sixty on the other, with five in no-mans' land in the middle. With all seats declared, there was still no government. This was the major parties' worst nightmare coming to fruition, a hung parliament. This could only mean that sooner or later, someone would be supplied with enough rope and the result would finally be known. It would not be pretty.

Chapter 3.
"The one who gives an answer before listening is both stupid and shameful."

Tuesday, 4th Mai, 1000.

Robert arrived in the office quite unexpectedly at just after half past seven. His new car had cut down the travel time from three hours to slightly less than an hour and a half, which meant that he was now sitting in the quiet.

The morning's newspapers were full of opinion pieces about who should form government but even they were at a loss to work out who actually would. As it stood, the battlelines were drawn wit sixty on one side and five dozen on the other; with five in no man's land. At some point, there would have to be negotiation before government could be formed.

In the quiet of the morning, Robert familiarised himself with parliamentary procedures and read through a list of the standing orders, most of which had not changed since the opening of democratic government. There were twelve leather bound volumes of law and procedure which came with the office and Robert assumed that it was expected of him that he at least would have read through them. No doubt that there were senior members on both sides of both chambers who could quote chapter and section from all of them.

By about half past eight, the faint rumblings of life could be heard through closed doors and Robert decided that he would have to steel himself before he found himself at the negotiation table. He was quite startled though, when the telephone which sat on his desk began to ring.

The Independent Member for Drusillica, Ivan Nilsson invited Robert to his office down on the fourth floor. Robert left via the inner door and immediately was aware that a large number of people had left their doors open; some were even watching him as he descended.

There were 240 offices in the central section of The Shortcake, arranged in a square with nine down the sides and offices in each of the corners. Just like the inner corridors, there were also lifts and stairwells which could only be reached via the inner doors of the various offices. Robert imagined that if you pulled the roof off of the building, that it would look a little like a Monopoly board and that he was given the office at Saint Basil's Station. Ivan Nilsson's office was one the other side of the board and almost directly opposite.

When Robert arrived in Ivan's office, the door was shut firmly behind him and there were already other members inside. "Come in, come in. As I've said, I'm Ivan Nilsson. This is Sophia Drazic; this is David Zoran and this is Marie Androva." "Good Morning."

Robert was directed to a seat, which he took and looked around the room. He thought that he was at least semi-familiar with politics but he very quickly realised that he knew no-one seated in the room. Ivan spoke:
"You're probably wondering why I've invited you all here. It will have dawned on you all by now that the election has returned a hung parliament – sixty to sixty. I'm here to tell you that the five people in this room will decide who governs this country for the next three years. There are one hundred and twenty five members in parliament and we are the five who will determine this country's fate. Now we can either all go together as a block and just announce who we will support or we can wait for the offers of the parties to see what they will give us in return for our support."

"We aren't a party," said Sophia. "You can't just drag us in here and demand that we'll all vote the same way. Who appointed you as leader anyway?"
"I am the Father of the House," said Ivan proudly.
"Even so," continued Sophia; the blood vessels in her temples beginning to beat furiously, "we might not even want to throw our support behind someone who we find abhorrent."

Sophia Drazic had been the Minister for Health in a previous KDP government. She had serious problems with the way that the KDP and then the ULP/SR governments had privatised the national telecommunications system and the national banking system and the national electricity boards; and had quit the party. She was now in her fifties and it was evident, even in this small gathering, that she would not be bullied into any decision lightly.

David, Marie and Robert were all newly elected members and had never served in the parliament before. Unlike Robert though, David and Marie had both served on local councils and Marie in particular was quite a skilled legal practitioner.

"What sort of political capital do we have?" asked David, playing with a pen idly.

"I suppose that it would depend on the sorts of concessions that the parties are prepared to make. Maybe they might appoint us to the cabinet but I really can't speak for what they may or may not do."

"What are you hoping to get out of this?" David prodded.

"What do you mean 'get out of this'?"

"Well, you must have had some reason for bringing us here like this. You obviously want something if you want us to hang together. You must fear hanging separately."

"I don't know what you mean."

"Claiming that you are Father of The House is one thing but does that imply that you want to be the guardian of the children?"

"Look here."

"Oh, I'm looking but I don't know what I see. Maybe you should explain yourself better. What you do want from this?"

"I just want the right people to take government."

"Who are 'the right people'?" Sophia chimed in.

"The right people… are not the wrong people."

Hush fell over the meeting. Robert could hear footsteps in the inner corridor. He got up out of his seat and stuck his head out to look. A lady at one end broke into double-step and quickly entered one of the offices.

"I think that someone might be watching our every move," offered Robert.

"I think that everyone will be watching our every move," concurred Sophia.

Robert couldn't help but notice that Marie Androva, who at thirty-two was easily the youngest of this quintet, had remained silent for the whole meeting. Her silence was deafening.
It was David who broke the silence, like a brick being hurled through a closed window.

"You still haven't said that what you hope to get out of this. It's all very well to say that the right people or the wrong people might take government but without telling us who you think that the right people or wrong people are, it is like you're expecting us to follow you blindly like the rats in Der Rattenfänger von Hameln or worse, the children. As the Father of the House who is expecting the little children to just follow him without question, you deny us the chance to think for ourselves.
How do we know that you're not leading us away from the town never to return?"

Ivan was visibly annoyed. He knew that Sophia Drazic wasn't likely to follow him because they had past history but he wasn't sure about David or Marie. He especially had no idea about Robert who had no political history at all.
David's brow furrowed. There was more than a hint of derision in his voice now.

"Suppose that the government absolutely had to be formed this afternoon, or else the King himself would close parliament and declare fresh elections. Whose side are you on?"
"Even now I am not at liberty to tell you."
"Then I no longer see the point of this meeting," announced David. He stood up, bowed politely and with all the low rumbling fury he could muster said "Good Day Sir."
"But – "
"I said Good Day!"

David left the room via the outer office and could be heard muttering to the press huddle waiting outside, who had been tipped off by someone else within the building. Sophia, Marie and Robert blinked at each other, slightly bemused.

"We've both kicked about this building for a while now. We know how the game works and we're not likely to be playing on the same side all that often. Why should we just blindly follow you?"

"I think that we're going to be more effective working as a block than we ever would separately."

"Do you intend to draw up a list of demands to present to the leaders?" quizzed Sophia.

"Do we need to be as formal as all of that?"

"Yes," said Sophia unequivocally, "I think that a formal document is certainly the way to go. We absolutely need a guarantee in writing of everyone's intent, so that we can hold them to it once government is formed. We don't want to hand over the proverbial blank cheque to whoever we finally side with."

As though he was hitting a road block, Ivan tried to press Marie and Robert into siding with him and steer around the problem.

"Well, what do you think," asked Ivan; leering at Robert.

"I don't know what to think. I think that it is wise to have an in principle list of demands but I don't really know what if anything that I need to demand."

"How about demanding tax cuts? People should be able to hold their own money without the government taking it away."

"If we cut taxes, then what? Someone has to pay to run the government. I don't think that we could argue for tax increases after an election."

"Then we should argue for the cutting of government waste."

"Did you read the last budget? People on pensions already lost out, relative to inflation. There are lots of government agencies which we understaffed and I don't know how you improve services with less money."

"We'll leave that there then."

Ivan appeared to grow bored with Robert and so tried to engage with Marie who looked quite intimidated.

"What about you? What sort of things would you want to see in list of demands, if we were to present that to the leaders of the two parties?"

Marie winced. "I don't want to be in this," she said before getting up and making her way to the door. "Thank you for your time." Marie bowed and closed the door quietly behind her as she left.

Ivan blinked at Sophia who rolled her eyes; Robert remained silent.

"What do you suppose that was about?"
"Are you ignorant as well as tactless, Ivan?"
Ivan scratched his beard; completely oblivious to what had just occurred. Robert felt uncomfortable and wanted to be let out and Sophia made her feelings felt.

"I don't care who you think you are, Ivan Nilsson. If you want to play your power games and manipulate people to your will, you're going to have to do better that this. If you but out your wish list, then I might decide to join you but not until then. With hope, I say good morning to you."
Sophia got up and left as well.

"I suppose that leaves us," said Ivan expectantly.
"Leaves us to do what?"
"Compile out list of demands."
"I don't know what I want yet. I don't really think that I'd be at all useful."

Robert also got up. He bowed and exited the room. Ivan wondered if his time had passed. Perhaps he was not the great inspiration that he thought he was.

Tuesday, 4th Mai, 1000.
In the parliamentary cafeteria at lunch time, there were a number of people quietly milling about, having their own talks about tactics. Robert had taken his lunch to work in a paper sack because he didn't think that paying more than a thousand Lek for a sandwich was in any way sane. He sat down by a window and watched as white fluffy cotton wool clouds danced and skipped behind the red curtains of a Chinese Flame Tree. He casually flipped through the morning's edition of Plotchki Pravda and saw that they were finally aware of his name and that he was one of the "gang of five" who would finally determine which side of the great divide would form government.

Robert was becoming aware that the people in the room were beginning to regard him from afar. As one of the gang of five, he would determine their fate. He was aware that he could see the whites of the eyes of people who would, depending on the outcome of his eventual decision, become his enemy and this did not sit well with him at all. Soon, after nine hundred ticks of the clock, he got up and left the cafeteria, the whites of those eyes burning like points of fire in his back.

As he walked down a corridor towards the block where the members' offices were, he was aware of even more stares from people and walking across the central courtyard, he looked up to see even more eyes, dart back inside their own offices.

Robert returned to his office and could hear murmuring on the other side of the door to the outer corridor. If he opened the door, then the press would likely invade; so he retreated through the central room to the inner office and locked both doors from the inside.

He was curious about who Ivan. David, Marie and Sophia would side with and surmised that only three of them were needed to finally tilt the table. He hoped that it would be three of them and that his decision didn't really matter in the end.

He considered his options.

He didn't really like the way that the KDP had carved up so many ex-government businesses and had sold off the silver in the trophy cabinet. He also didn't like the way that the KDP had introduced a Value Added Tax which had the effect of falling more heavily on poorer people, which included the old and disabled.

He didn't like the way that United Labour had rung up so much debt in the term before last that the number was so big that it didn't have a proper name. Twenty trillion Lek? A trillion wasn't a number that his brain could even hold efficiently – anything with twelve zeroes just looked like the response that an audience at a pantomime might give: "Ooooooh".

He also didn't know what the point of the Socialist Robots actually was. Democracy had come and there was no way that people were going to consider going back to the way things were and yet during this election, their numbers had actually increased. That meant that more people had voted for them.

It was too confusing. Robert thought about the problem and tried to pull it apart in his mind but it was like a big ball of tangled wire. You could roll the ball around forever and still not find a way to untangle it.

He thought about the "gang of five" and decided to log on to the internal email system. Hopefully the lists of phone numbers of all the candidates would be published by now and he could ask the other four in turn, who they would be supporting. After a short period of time when his computer displayed a spinning cartwheel, he found a few emails from parliamentary admin. He thought about printing out a list of phone numbers but realised that his office had not been furnished with a printer. Would he have to request one of those or would he have to buy one? There was a certain elegance about the phone numbers of parliamentary members. Robert's number ended in 615 which was also his office number and it was the same for every Member of Parliament – the room number went with the office. The list also included the name of the electorate which the member represented and Robert thought that that might be helpful in guessing how the other four would go.

Unfortunately, all the other four candidates represented rural electorates and this in itself made guessing difficult. Unlike city electorates where you could mostly guess how the population was likely to vote, based purely on postcode, in the country, the rules were entirely different. Rural electorates were either so staunchly leftist that they made the old communists look progressive or so staunchly rightist that they made even laissez-faire fans look like a Sunday School picnic.

He looked online and found election results going all the way back to the very first parliament and found that all five electorates of the independents (including his own) were so wildly erratic that even trying to pick a winner on the basis of swing, was a nonsense.

There was only one thing for it. He would have meet with all of them.

He dialled Ivan Nilsson's number but it was busy. He phoned David Zoran's number but it too was busy. Marie Androva's number was not busy but it dialled out. Sophia Drazic's number was not busy; it did not dial out; there was an actual person at the other end. Sophia's secretary answered the phone and promised that Sophia would be back within ten minutes; so she would be free to hold a meeting in half an hour's time.
Robert went back to the central room in his office and watched the news.

Tuesday, 4th Mai, 1000.
Like Ivan's, David's and even his own office, Sophia Drazic's office also ended in the number 5. Robert's office was number 615 and Sophia's was two floors down at 415. Ivan and David's were 435 and 535 respectively. Robert was beginning to suspect something, for it always seemed as though the major parties knew where he was going at most times. He thought that he would put that question to Sophia.

Sophia had been a member since the second parliament; which meant that she was only second to Ivan Nilsson in terms of period served. Her office, which she had occupied since the year 983, had a well lived in look about it. Unlike Robert's grim and stark furniture, Sophia's was all deep mahogany and most of the fittings were made from brass. Even the electric kettle which she kept in the central room was made from a coppery metal which glowed the same rich earthy tones as the rest of the decor.
The only concession to the tenth and soon to be eleventh century was the flat screen television which stood in the middle room and her laptop which was a pearlescent white.
Robert was directed into the outer room by Sophia's secretary; who duly came back with a tea set before disappearing to the inner room of the office.

"Good Morning Mister Ilanyich, I trust that you've been able to keep the media pack at bay."
"Yes, ma'am."
"Good. Good... tea?"
"Yes please."
Sophia poured just a lick of milk into the cups before pouring in the tea. The tea danced and swirled as though a storm was brewing before settling down to a uniform tan colour.

"Now then, what was it that you wanted to see me about?"
"I just have a feeling that this is all just a strange sort of game."
"How so?"
"There are five independents and so everyone says that we're the ones who are the kingmakers."
"That's correct."
"But there are eight members of the Socialist Robot Party. If they decided that they'd like to support the KDP instead of United Labour, then all the negotiation that we'll end up doing is completely pointless."

Robert looked worried. Sophia smiled at him and looked vacantly into her cup of tea. She had seen this sort of worry before and knew the implications of the situation far better than anyone would have suspected.

"Mister Ilanyich," started Sophia, "what you've said is utterly correct except for one thing."
"What's that?"
"The Robots will never side with the KDP."

Robert looked stunned. Sophia continued.

"The Socialist Robots get their name from the word 'robota' which means 'hard work' in Czech. They sit even further to the economic left than the United Labour Party.
The Socialist Robots would like to go even further than United Labour in that, not only are they asking for better conditions for workers, particularly in factories, but they would also like it if the ownership of those factories were turned over to worker's collectives."
"Like the old communists?"
"Not exactly. The communists wanted to have all economic assets owned by the state but the Socialist Robots want things owned directly by the workers themselves.

Both the KDP and United Labour have over the past twenty years, privatised no end of state owned businesses and assets and the Socialist Robots have opposed every single proposal to the hilt. Even when they have been in government with United Labour, it has been an uneasy coalition, with the Robots voting against many policies. In those times, United Labour was helped by the KDP in passing legislation."

Robert pondered this for a moment. It meant that eventually, he would be forced to choose a side. The depth of the responsibility began to yawn upon him like a chasm which was ready to swallow him whole.

"I have finished with the KDP. Ivan can say all that he likes but he knows that I can't forgive the party for what they've done. He will be looking for an answer and will probably want me to side with the KDP like he always does but he's fighting a losing battle.
It hasn't been said yet but we both know that the race isn't sixty to sixty like everyone thinks that it is but sixty-one to sixty-one."
"Who do you think that I should throw my hat in the ring with?"
"I think that we'd be better served by a Labour-Robot government but you need to do what's best for the people who elected you."

They continued to chat for a while about this and that; about that and this and when the tea had finished, Robert took his leave and left via the inner door. The prying eyes of politicians were calmer than the media scrum waiting outside in the outer corridors.

Chapter 4.
"A wise man makes his own decisions, an ignorant man follows the public opinion."

Wednesday, 5th Mai, 1000.
The problem with making any decision is always the gaping void of doubt when you consider what the alternative is. Economists have the handy term of 'opportunity cost' when taking about such matters but what happens if the choice forgone does not and can not possibly be quantified into anything resembling rational units? How do you for instance make sense of the political capital which was surrendered as result of your decision? Robert thought about this and the idea spun around inside his mind as though it were a marble trapped inside a balloon. If he chose one, he could not choose the other - they were mutually exclusive.

There weren't any meaningful emails which demanded Robert's attention and as far as speaking to anyone from the major parties was concerned, that trail had gone cold. With nothing to do, Robert decided to go for a walk.

The Shortcake was a rabbit warren of a building at the best of times and at the moment, it was positively chaotic. New members of parliament were having their offices fitted out and tradespeople were coming and going all the time. This invariably put a strain on the security staff in the building and longer than normal queues were forming at all the major security checkpoints.

Robert walked into the public gallery and saw two lines of school children being led by a lady in a special parliamentary blazer and their two teachers, who were probably just glad to be out of the classroom, tagged along behind the stragglers.

Robert bought a copy of The Plotchki, which was the newspaper of conservatives and to his horror, he found himself the subject of ridicule and contempt in an editorial on page 18.

"Mr. Ilanyich has the power to make or break the government and the power to single-handedly set the course of Plotchkan politics back a generation. Virtually no-one knows who this shadowy man is and having worked previously in the manufacturing sector, it is thus paper's opinion that the man cannot be trusted either. He may very well harbour latent Marxist or Socialist ideas and we simply do not trust him. He might be the sort who squirrels his way into organisations and destroys then from the inside. Such people are a national security risk and are an enemy of democracy itself."

Robert was shocked.
How could the newspaper even get away with it? By saying expressly that this was only the paper's 'opinion' they covering their backs because they weren't necessarily bound by the code of conduct for journalism. There were remedies for outright errors in fact but newspapers like the general public were free to publish any opinion they liked; only the laws of defamation stood against them and defamation was incredibly difficult to prosecute.

He stood up with an anger burning white hot but with no outlet to release it. He could feel his hands throbbing, so he walked over to the fountain in the middle of the lobby and dipped his hands in the cool water.
Almost immediately, three children broke free of their two straight lines and also put their hands in the fountain. Fearing a mass revolt, their tour group leader walked the rest of them over and soon there were twenty-six children; all standing around with wet hands.

"I'm sorry for all this noise and trouble," said an embarrassed looking teacher.
"Oh that's all right. Children will be children."
"As you can imagine, trying to control twenty-six children can be difficult at times. Sometimes it's a bit like the madness that goes on inside those parliamentary chambers in there."

Robert wasn't sure if he should say that he was a new member of 'those parliamentary chambers in there' because he didn't know if that would illicit praise, curiosity or scorn. It didn't matter though, for off in the distance their tour guide was already calling them to move on. The opportunity cost of becoming an MP was a quiet life, free from the nation's opinions.

Wednesday, 5th Mai, 1000.
Sometime later after Robert had had his official photograph taken for the parliamentary website and government directories, he returned to his office and the mind numbing quiet hush of the white noise of the air conditioning. There are some days when doing nothing is all that you want to do but even that begins to pall eventually. No-one would return his phone calls and no-one really seemed to care if he was there at all.
Finally, there was a knock at the door but instead of someone wanting to see him, they apologised for disturbing him.

"Oh, I'm sorry. I'd quite forgotten that Mister Khan no longer occupies this office."
"That's all right."
"You must be his replacement. That is such a pity."
"Oh."

The accidental intruder thrust out her hand to shake Robert's. She was a relatively tall lady with ovaloid spectacles and she looked as though she might be the sort of person who ran a library with ruthless efficiency. She had straight, cherry ginger hair, which itself was interesting as almost nobody in Plotchka had ginger hair.

"Don't be offended," she said, "my name is Sarai Glickova; Member for Trajanus and also the KDP. You can understand why I'm a little disappointed to see you here."
"I suppose."
"Don't get me wrong, you're probably a perfectly nice person but my minders wouldn't like me speaking with the enemy, as it were."
"The enemy? Oh, I'm not a member of either the Robots or Labour. I'm an independent."
"Yes! That's right. You're that guy, aren't you? You're that indie who still hasn't declared his allegiance."

"Ha ha, that would be me. Robert Ilanyich is the name. I am that indie."

"Well you probably should be aware that although we are free to talk to anyone in the building we wish, generally speaking, we don't. The party whips like to know who has been talking to who and what sort of discussions have been had. One of the downsides of party based politics is that there are people who make strategies and work out what can be negotiated for. If you want to further your career and become anything important, you kind of have to play by the rules. If you strike out on your own and play where you shouldn't be playing, that gets back to the whips and they then start looking for people whose loyalty can be trusted."

"I see."

"Even the news that we've had this conversation will probably make its way back to the whip's office at some stage and I'm more than likely going to have to come up with some sort of excuse as to why I was in here. This morning I can probably get away with saying that I was extending the hand of friendship with the purpose of eventually securing your support but if this was in say, six or seven months' time, then I doubt whether I'd have even been in here for this long."

"Thanks, I think. But why are you telling me this? Isn't it in your best interest that I should remain as naive as possible, as to his the system works?"

"More than likely. You have to remember though, that in this place, not only do we have the enemies of the opposition but we also have the enemies of the press and the civil service. This place is nasty enough without needing to deliberately make it more so."

"Thanks for being human."

"Don't mention it," said Sarai; the words loaded with double meaning. "I'm afraid I must be on my way now. The party machines don't like to work if the cogs aren't aligned properly. Maybe we'll speak again under different circumstances but they'd have to be vastly different."

Sarai exited the office; leaving Robert even more alone. When he was working in the washing machine factory, although the people there weren't exactly his friends, they weren't his enemies either. In here, people were formally declared enemies in a perpetual war; for the moment, Robert was standing in no man's land.

Thursday, 6th Mai, 1000.

The general silence continued. Whenever Robert tried to phone anyone from either side, the telephone calls were either being accepted by parliamentary secretaries or would go through to voice mail. Robert found this incredibly frustrating and not at all helpful.

The problem was its own vicious cycle - members could not be contacted because they weren't immediately required; so they either didn't arrive in their offices or didn't take phone calls and because they either didn't arrive in their offices or didn't take phone calls, they could not be contacted. Trying to negotiate with a wall of silence is a fruitless task.

Robert took to reading parliamentary notices from the previous term and also decided that sitting in the outer corridor might be more conducive to communicating with... anyone really.

In the previous term, Anton Diakonos' government had tried to pass legislation which would have allowed the two state television stations Channel 5 and 5A to carry advertising. Although this had passed through the Commune Assembly, the house of fruits and nuts (the Senate) had blocked passage of the bill. Technically, the Prime Minister could have called for a petition to be sent to the king to dissolve both houses of parliament, call a full election and have a joint sitting on the bill but now that the election had been held according to the normal rules, that opportunity would be lost.

On top of that, the only way that it could happen again would be if that same bill was also passed by the Commune Assembly and rejected thrice by the Senate; thus going around the merry-go-round again. At the moment, without a formal government to introduce any bills, the merry-go-round had broken down entirely.

Robert had thought that Channel 5 and 5A should help to pay their own way and carry advertising and so if he was going to support the KDP to form government, then that would be a piece of legislation which he would help to pass. Again, with no formal government, this could not even happen.

So for a portion of Thursday morning, Robert sat in the outer corridor, watching people in suits and jackets walk past. Mostly they were junior staff, presumably preparing documents for the upcoming term of parliament when it would be finally declared.

At just after half-past ten, when he was reading through at a series of discussions to do with the very late passage of the Appropriation Bills Act 999 and the arguments which nearly saw the government collapse due to an outright collapse of supply, he didn't even notice a gentleman sit down in the seat on the other side of the low table he was sitting next to.

"I don't think that we're going to get much sunshine today, old boy."
"Huh?"
"I say, it looks kind of grey and horrid out there. We'd be well advised to stay indoors today."

Robert looked up from the book he was reading. Sitting opposite was Anwar Ul-Haq, the United Labour Party's shadow Exchequer.

"I'm sorry, I didn't notice you there."
"Not to worry. We often get quite engrossed in what we're reading. I note that you're reading through last year's parliamentary bulletins and notes. That's quite a good idea. I don't know if any of us can keep completely up to speed on what passes through here."
"I thought that I'd better get some reading done whilst there was a bit of a lull. I can't seem to get hold of anyone to talk to."
"Ah, no. You see, I'm afraid that the party whips have us well... whipped."
"My problem is that I hold one of the last votes to decide who does form government and no-one has been all that willing to set up any meetings to discuss things."
"You'll find that around here. No-one likes to discuss things with people who have the potential to become a future enemy."

That made Robert think. Anwar made sense. For someone to speak to him, they would invariably have to give away an idea of what their upcoming policy agenda would be. That sort of information had the potential to be leaked and because the ship of state is the only ship which leaks from the top first and from the inside out, plugging the holes did not mean trying to stop people from getting in but information from getting out.

It was a strange sort of paradox. Politics is about the selling ideas but the problem with an idea is that once it escapes, it can't be nailed down. Ideas can be appropriated, thought through, improved and then made one's own. As the currency of democracy, giving away ideas is like giving away money; no-one particularly likes that.

Anwar spoke again.

"You know, this might sound really silly but once we leave the confines of this crazy pressure cooker, many of us are pretty easy going when we don't have to talk shop. You might not end up having your most critical conversations in this building but outside.
Three hundred years ago, the political discussions which turned the fate of nations, took place in coffee houses and public houses. Even one hundred and seventy five years ago, the 'scrap of paper' which created Belgium out of thin air, was probably thought out in a coffee house in London. You can just imagine Charles Dickens sitting over in a corner, muttering to himself like a mad man, whilst other people were drawing black lines on the map of Europe.
Lots of people have read Nicholas Nickleby but almost no-one has read the Treaty of London."

Robert had read neither Nicholas Nickleby nor the Treaty of London but assumed that both of them must have been interesting pieces of fiction in their own way: literary and legal.

"The one truly important thing to remember about this place is that it is a house of elephants," continued Anwar, "and elephants never forgive."
"Don't you mean 'forget'?"
"Everyone thinks that but it is wrong. Elephants can't remember what they had for breakfast. On the other hand, if an elephant thinks that you have wronged it; even if all the reasons are wrong; even if there are no real reasons; even if the elephant's recollection is totally faulty and that thing absolutely never ever had even the possibility of happening, they'll come around to your place and stomp your house into the ground."
"Really?" asked Robert with suspicion.

"No not really. If elephants were that smart, they wouldn't allow their feet to be turned into umbrella stands."

Friday, 7th Mai, 1000.
Friday in Plotchka was the day that the three weekly state newspapers were published. Back in the days of the communists, they came out daily and were the only officially allowed newspapers. Since the advent of democracy and the deregulation of the press, their budgets were pared back severely and now they only came out once a week; shadows of their former selves. Futuris was the newspaper of record and it published all court notices and official statistics. When there were state businesses, Futuris would also collect and report production statistics, though the general public was suspicious about the figures being reported. It was hard to accept month after month of record production figures when supermarkets often had shortages. These days, Futuris was heavily used by private companies writing promotional puff pieces thinly disguised as news items.

Robert was sitting at his desk when a reporter from Futuris arrived to interview him. She was not particularly interested in being there.
Both Robert and the reporter knew (though they didn't say so) that they only reason that she was there was to grab a scoop before anyone else. She had used the pretext that she was writing a "meet your Member of Parliament" feature; which the paper had run from time to time on particularly slow news weeks. As she conducted the interview though, her apathy grew ever more apparently when she learned that unlike more colourful members of parliament, Robert's previous job had been in a washing machine factory and that he had been happily married for almost twenty years. These things did not shift copy.

Suddenly, her mobile phone rang and Robert could hear an immediate change in her tone. She became very excited about the message that she'd just heard and immediately apologised, got up and ran down the corridor at full tilt.
Robert deduced that something interesting must be happening and so he closed the outer door to his offices and switched on the television.

Marie Androva and Ivan Nilsson were addressing the media and announcing that they were going to give their support to the KDP on issues of supply on the floor of the Commune Assembly. Officially this put the count at sixty-two to sixty but Robert remembered that Sophia Drazic would not follow suit and so the actual count stood at sixty-two to sixty-one. The only two unaligned members of the Commune Assembly were David Zoran and Robert. The next question was who David would support but Robert didn't have to wait terribly long for his answer because the phone rang and David was on the other end of the line, asking Robert to visit him in his office immediately. Robert agreed.

As Robert walked down the internal corridor to David's office, he noticed that practically every television in the building was carrying Channel 5A's feed of Ivan and Marie who were now with the still incumbent Prime Minister Anton Diakonos. In front of them was a very official looking treaty and by the time that Robert reached David's office, the agreement was signed. David stood in his doorway and was keen to usher Robert inside; fearful of the myriad of eyes that might be watching.

"I suppose that you've seen the news by now," said David redundantly.
"Yes, I have."
"You know what that means?"
"No."
"It means that Marie caved in. That's what it means."
"Caved in?"

David tried to hold back his frustration; unsuccessfully. It was obvious what his intention was and he was not afraid of expressing it.

"You know what this means? It means that we have to move quickly to make our own agreement to join the Robots and Labour."
"Does it?"
"It means… wait a minute. You haven't said who you intend to support yet, have you?"
"Actually, I haven't decided."

David paused to regather his thoughts. In his sound and fury, he hadn't considered the possibility that Robert hadn't yet made up his mind. He just assumed that Robert felt the same way as he did. He changed his approach.

"If you don't support the Robots and Labour, we'll be stuck with a KDP government for three more years."
"And if I do, we'll be stuck with a Labour/Robot coalition for the next three years."
"Shouldn't you just pick the lesser of two evils?"
"I'd rather not pick any evils. If the choice is between radish and garlic when what you want is ice cream, why can't you ask for something else?"
"Because there is no 'something else'. If you want fruits and nuts, look in the Senate. It's full of them."

Robert's dilemma came into full focus. It was bad enough being at the ballot box and not knowing who to vote for when faced with an unpalatable choice but the people had chosen and they were divided. The fate of the government itself now hung upon Robert's choice; it was the single most difficult choice that he ever had to face.
Marrying Katherine was an easy choice. Buying their apartment whilst extremely disappointing was also a relatively simple choice. Even buying a new car although it was a choice with many valid outcomes, was still an easy choice to make. This choice was hard.

"I think that I'd like more time to consider this."
"Well when you do make up your mind, make sure that you make up your mind properly and make the right choice."
"Okay."
"Don't you dare make the wrong choice. If you do, you'll have no but yourself to blame and believe me, everyone in the whole country and especially me, will want to blame you for making the wrong choice."

Seeing as this meeting would not produce anything more productive, Robert took his leave. As he walked back down the corridor to his office, he passed several people but thought little of it. They had very much had vested interest in the choice that he would make and their fate would be decided one way or the other.

If he had been paying careful attention to the sounds that were going on around him, telephones began to rang and doors started to slam shut. The internal corridors became very quiet as Robert made his way back to his office but he thought nothing of it.

He made his way back to his desk and took a seat. There was a knock at the door. Robert assumed that it must be the mail service as it was about that time of the morning but he couldn't have been further from the truth.

As Robert opened the door, a surge of television cameras, people with microphones and clipboards all burst into the room.

Robert returned to his desk and saw six cameras with their anonymous grey eyes staring back at him. There must have been at least a dozen microphones from various news outlets. It was as if a pack of sharks wanted to stop and admire a haddock before they ripped it asunder.

"Who did you speak to David Zoran about?"
"Who will you be supporting to form government?"
"What has either side offered you thus far?"
"Who do you think will be the next Prime Minister?"

Questions came at him like rapid fire from a belt-fed machine gun and were about as subtle. Robert felt like a dormouse that had somehow wandered into no man's land on the Western Front and was now caught in spotlights from both entrenched sides.

He attempted to speak.

"Um..."

Immediately the barrage of questions stopped. The guns fell silent.

The flashes continued and motor gears whirred balefully but it was as if someone had called 'set' in a footrace and the starter was holding their firing pistol aloft.

Robert surveyed the crowd in front of him. His fortieth birthday had come and passed and was little more than an entry in a long discarded desk diary; his temples were now painted in silver. The lackeys in front of him were on average just over barely half his age and life and experience had not yet been kicked the impetuousness of youth out of them.

He realised that they had all the tact of a dozen Dobermans and that if he were to throw even the tiniest of morsels to them, they would chase it down and rip it to pieces.

He folded his hands on the desk in front of him and closed his eyes. He could still hear the whirr of electric motors but now he could hear the white noise from the air conditioning as well.

He spoke slowly and quietly.

"I have not spoken with either leader of either of the main parties. I do not yet know who I will support to form government. I have not as yet been offered anything and I do not know what if anything I will be offered. That is all."

Robert opened a desk drawer and pulled out a thermos and a paper sack. Somewhere down the hallway, a clock chimed off eleven times.

"Now, if you'll excuse me, I have a scheduled meeting with a ham sandwich."

Robert got to his feet, took his thermos and paper sack with him walked to the door of his office, waited until everyone had got out, locked the door and strode back through the outer corridor to the public gallery. He left The Shortcake through the front main entrance and walked towards a public park, still be followed by reporters with cameras.

He arrived at a park bench and took out a ham sandwich and a paperback novel. The reporters gradually lost interest and one by one, they left him in peace.

When Robert returned from lunch he entered The Shortcake via the secure car park underneath the building and locked the outer door to his office. He tried to phone both the leaders of the KDP and United Labour but neither of them were there to take his call.

He decided to familiarise himself with parliamentary procedure and read through the standing orders for the Commune Assembly. The rest of the afternoon was relatively quiet and there were no more knocks at the door.

Robert spent the afternoon replying to correspondence; which also included a request for a meeting from a primary school for a group of fifth grade students. It was strange to think that when he was a boy, there would never have been a school field trip to parliament because the communists were decidedly more unfriendly than either side of politics today.

Eventually five o'clock rolled around and Robert decided to go home. He also decided to leave via the inner office and corridors just in case the media wanted to pursue him again.

Friday, 7th Mai, 1000.

One advantage about living in the east of any country or city is that when you make your travels to and from work, the sun is forever at your back. Robert pitied the poor saps who lived in the west, as twice daily the sun would be in their eyes.

There had been an afternoon storm which washed the roads clean and with the sun behind him, it was as if the house lights were upon some vast stage. The whole vault of the heavens was a vast set of curtains, set in grey velvet.

Traffic on the M3 was still furious and a lime green Italian motorway burner buzzed past as though the whole world were its racetrack. Robert was content to sit at 120, knowing full well that this was faster than his previous car could ever achieve.

Curiously there were an abnormally large number of black four wheel drive cars on the motorway and more than a few of them took the same motorway exit as he did.

When the news fanfare came over the radio for the seven o'clock news, Robert arrived at his apartment block and found that the swarm of cameras and microphones was already there to meet him. He forced his way through a jostling crowd and took the elevator up to his apartment to find that Katherine was not at all happy. She flung her arms around him and kissed him, much to his confused amazement.

"I thought that the worst had happened."
"What?"
"I don't know what."
"Wait. What?"

Katherine went into the kitchen and came back with the imaginatively named afternoon newspaper "Afternoon." It had a picture of Robert eating his ham sandwich in the park and bore the headline "Government Ham Sandwiched".

"I thought maybe someone wanted to kill you."
"Wait, hang on. What?"
"The TV news has been following you all the way home. I thought maybe you'd committed some heinous crime."
"Well… I practically have."

Katherine raged.

"Robert Ian Ilanyich, you tell me this instant what you've done to have the media chase you down like a dog, or else you'll have me to answer to."
"Well…"
"Spit it out. Now!"
"I haven't made a decision."

Katherine's rage stopped. She was still angry but now she wanted to know what Robert had to say for himself.

"Go on."

"We still don't have a government in this country, a week after the election. I think that there are probably going to be sixty-two on one side and sixty-two on the other which leaves me in the middle and everyone wants to know who I'm going to choose and I have no idea who I'm going to choose because it's so very hard when I don't really like either side and everyone wants to know now; if not yesterday."

Katherine suddenly felt very sorry for Robert.

This was her Robert who found it difficult to decide from a menu in a restaurant. This was her Robert who didn't like sitting towards the front of their church because he didn't like people staring at the bald patch on the back of his head. This was her Robert who had accidentally clogged the toilet when he had tried to fix it. This was her nervous Robert who accidentally became a member of parliament because he thought it was an interesting scheme to make some money for free.

This was her Robert who not only had to make a difficult decision which affected the nation but he had to do so with the prying eyes of the nation looking on.

"Tomorrow is Saturday, Rob. We'll go down to the hardware store and buy some hinges for the kitchen cabinets. We'll to the garden centre and see if we can get something to perk up the aspidistra. You won't have me to answer to; you won't have anyone to answer to. Tomorrow is Saturday, the nation can wait for all I care."

Saturday, 8th Mai, 1000.
A week out from the election, Robert sat on his sixth storey apartment balcony and gazed over the city. Harlequin and Columbine were never allowed outside, for fear that the law of gravity was unkind to those who fell afoul of it; it was very quick to prosecute. From up here you could see almost the entire of Astari.

Astari was like lots of other cities which had been developed whilst the Iron Curtain was draped over eastern Europe. Unlike the grander cities of western Europe like Paris or London where the experiments of people like Le Corbusier utilised concrete for art's sake, the concrete constructs of the communists were just cheap and nasty. Now fifty or sixty years on, they added dangerous and unsound to cheap and nasty. No-one would miss their passing if they were demolished.

Katherine had taken a bus downtown and would return (hopefully) with a new car; paid for by the remainder of Robert's parliamentary car allowance. He hoped that she would choose either a German or British car because there was at least a fair chance that it would have been built properly. He also hoped that it would be diesel or small or both.

Plotchka had to import all of its petrol, all of its natural gas and almost all of its coal. Some of its electricity came from nuclear power stations but thanks Chernobyl in the Ukraine and more recently Fukushima in Japan, people carried uneasy memories reminding them of the nuclear bogeyman.

Gas came via pipelines through the Ukraine and Romania and if the Ukraine hadn't paid its gas bills and if Romanian gas workers had chaotically decided to go on strike again, people would either freeze in their apartments or have to find other ways to cook dinner.

Plotchka bought its petrol where ever it could but because it had no pipelines of its own, the price remained at or above three-hundred Lek per litre which was amongst the most expensive in Europe.

Somewhere off in the distance, the town hall clock chimed off the half-hour into the still air and Robert could hear some shrikes who had built their nest on the roof, five storeys above. Way down below, Katherine called out to Robert from the street and instead of taking the elevator; he bounded down the six flights of stairs to street level. When he got downstairs he was pleased to see that Katherine had bought a German hatchback which was both diesel and small.

The thought also struck him that the media herd which had followed him home was not in attendance. Robert threw his arms wide and as soon as Katherine stepped out of the car he embraced her and swung her about on the spot.

"A week ago, I was sweeping the apartment like I do every Saturday whilst you were off playing tennis. Today, I don't care what needs doing. This is a great weekend."

"Nyet!"

"What?"

"Bozhe moi. I forgot to tell them that I wouldn't be at tennis today."

"Oh."

"Not to worry. I don't think they'll mind though. It's not like we're playing in a tournament or anything."

Katherine's new car was named after a powerful desert wind. Most cars in that range were named after winds. This was better than the name of the cars which originally came out of the factory which in German were called Strength Through Joy Wagons. If as a poet once said that living well is the best revenge, then the Germans had exacted their revenge very well indeed by selling so many Strength Through Joy Wagons that the company was among the largest in the world.

The car had electric everything, which was a departure from Katherine's previous car which didn't even have a radio. It had electric mirrors, electric windows, cruise control, traction control and it even had a feature which dimmed the lights like a movie theatre did, after you'd closed the doors. It was a totally pointless feature but one which Katherine tested again and again merely because she could.

Popular myth and wisdom suggested that the reason that the Cold War was eventually ended and communism lost was that the weapons used were things like silly putty, fizzy soft drink, instant custard, television dinners and boy bands. The communists failed because they learned that controlling people's consumption and desires was like herding cats – possible but futile.

Katherine pouted and decided that they should take a drive in her new car away from the city.

The motorways crossed the landscape like grey ribbons dragged over a pile of laundry but once you'd left them, there were many woodlands to explore and because it was Mai, many delicate spring flowers in the high country which made their annual display.

After leaving the M3 and they A34, they were now meandering down the B346. Robert wondered if people's driveways were according to the law technically roads and did they have their own secret numbers like F346152? If so, did that mean that the government could put a bus stop in the middle of your living room? Probably.

Eventually they stopped at a small café that looked as though hardly anyone ever visited it. There was a cheery fire, glowing away in an old stone fireplace and a scratchy record was playing on a gramophone. They were one hundred and six miles from home but a million miles from care, or whatever the metric equivalent was, Katherine declared.

After a nice meal of sandwiches, coffee and cake, the bill came to 1633 Lek and Robert left a two thousand Lek note on the table.

"What're you doing man? Don't you know how tight money is?" snapped Katherine.

"Is it?" Robert seemed apathetic.

"Do you even know how much money is in the bank?"

"Do you even know how much money is in the bank? Go on; check."

Katherine pulled out her mobile phone and stabbed and pecked and poked at it; muttering obscenities under her breath. She logged onto the internet banking website to check the balance but was confused and unable to comprehend the number staring back at her.

"How much are they paying you?"

"A little over twelve million a year."

"Twelve million?!"

Robert's previous job at the washing machine factory had paid just over four million Lek a year; whist Katherine's job at the print shop paid three and a half million. Being a parliamentarian was worth considerably more than both of their previous salaries combined.

"Robert," said Katherine "You do realise that if you are paid this much, then that must mean that the next three years are going to be harder for you? Your current decision whilst difficult is only the beginning. There might be many many more."
"I know."

They got back into the car and continued to eat away the miles. Robert remained quiet, having been reminded of the choice which was still impending. For the moment though, it would remain on hold. No decision however great could hope to compete with the majesty of the scenery opening before them. As the road rose over peaks and descended into valleys it sort of faded into the background.

They drove to a lookout, atop a ridge and overlooking a very wide tree-lined valley. Even though there was no-one else about, neither of them dared speak a word. All of creation yelling its heart out, drowned out all other voices; there was simply no need to speak and no words to be said.

"I want ice cream."
"Me too."

Sunday, 9th Mai, 1000.

After the fall of communism throughout Eastern Europe, religion began to take back the gains that it had been forced to give up. Grand church buildings which had remained dormant for fifty years, regained their vibrancy and their life and communities of believers sprang up in those places again. Katherine came from a family which even during the worst of the purges, never ever lost their faith but Robert arrived with fresh eyes and saw the bible firstly as an interesting explanation of why the world works the way it does and then as a living document. God was in charge, mankind was base, Jesus stepped into it and the church was the community of believers trying to live that out.

Robert was incredibly confused though, why in living out the tenants of faith, did the priesthood need to wear garb which was decidedly medieval and looked like something from an elaborate chess board. How could anything call itself orthodox when it looked so incredibly strange? Granted that for most of the week, when the priests and elders would go out and do genuine pastoral care in a world that predominantly didn't, that it was both necessary and noble, it still didn't explain why someone on Wednesday who might be seen visiting people who needed a friend or be out serving people in ways like mowing lawns, would on Sunday, dress up like St Nicholas.

Church music was something that stretched back hundreds of years and was still being written, which was natural for a people demanding to know and be known by their creator, but why did some of it have to be so naff?

After the service had ended, Robert and Katherine were on their way home after milling about with people when the priest came up to Robert. He seemed disinterested in Katherine.

"I understand that it is going to come down to your opinion on who decides who forms the next government."

"Yes, that's correct."

"Can you please choose the KDP? When it comes to matters like abortion and marriage, they're the ones who stand up for these things."

"I'll consider that."

"Thank you."

Robert wasn't entirely sure about that. The KDP which liked to picture itself as the party of business and the establishment, tended to either ignore social issues entirely or rallied the religious right behind it when it was expedient to do so. The KDP had in the past cut social welfare programs and during the past three years, old age pensions had been frozen and education budgets had been cut - they liked to tout cuts as "savings measures". Also, it was the KDP who have originally passed legislation which installed the VAT, which had the effect of taxing poorer people more. Parading words like 'abortion' and 'marriage' once every three years was rather like banging a loud gong or clanging a pair of cymbal. It all sounded a bit hollow.

Robert and Katherine continued on their way home. In the car, Robert considered that neither party had particularly said very much about those issues in their policy speeches and both parties were also silent in their manifestos. Besides which, the KDP and Labour were both pretty poor when it came to having a social conscious on issues to do with addressing real poverty. Only the Robots had come close to suggesting that people had a right to live frugal comfort as a result of the work of their hands. Why the priest would say something in favour of one party or another baffled Robert.

Chapter 5.
"Without counsel purposes are disappointed: but in the multitude of counsellors they are established.

Monday, 10th Mai, 1000.

Sleep was a pointless pursuit. As Robert lay staring at the ceiling, the clock in the hallway chimed off three o'clock. He got up very quietly so as not to disturb Katherine and decided to make a list of every reason why he ought to support one side or the other.

The KDP had privatised the Tigr Motor Company, the National Airports Commission, Plotchka Gas, Plotchka Dinamo, Plotchka Telekoms and the National Water Companies.

United Labour had privatised the Imperial Bank, The Postal Commission, the National Mapping Service, Air Plotchki and Plotchka State Railways.

His list grew and grew, Robert had grievances with the flotation of the Lek, wage cases, the way that the media companies had so much power, tariff reductions which had killed off national industries, the fact that investment companies now owned private housing and this and that and that and this and the other and it went on and on.

Pretty soon, tiredness began to return and he started back at his poor tortured piece of paper. His list came to sixty-two to sixty-two. Not even his list of complaints from his own brain was enough to swing his decision either way.

On his trip to work in the morning, callers to talkback radio were increasingly annoyed at the inability of the parliament to form government. The radio announcer openly called Robert a troublemaker on national radio and so when Robert arrived at the office, he was in a pretty foul mood.

His patience was running out and he decided to ring the party whips for both the KDP and United Labour but was surprised at their lack of enthusiasm to want to set up any sort of meeting at all. Eventually he organised meetings with the Chief Exchequer Edvard Michalic and his opposite in the shadow cabinet, Anwar Ul-Huq.

There was something intrinsically amusing about the term "shadow". It almost implied that there was a secretive and shady underworld in politics. If there wasn't a Shadow Vice Minister for Gambling, Liquor, Racing, Gaming and Hospitality then there should be. Such a person should also be required to have 'exotic' underworld connections and be a 'colourful' figure. That certainly would make Channel 5A's eleven o'clock news more entertaining.

Chief Exchequer Edvard Michalic was a deft player of the political game and had been moving pieces about the board for longer than Robert had been alive. This septuagenarian not only knew the value of a Lek, he probably also used to find ways of conning kids out of pfennigs in the school yard when he was a boy. Pfennigs were long gone; Edvard Michalic was for most intents and purposes, close to eternal.

Robert was led into an office which had the same floor plan as his own (as most offices did) but Edvard's was fusty. The portraits which hung on the wall dated from before the formation of the modern KDP and very much gave away that Edvard had been part of the old system.
Edvard led Robert into the room between the two offices and locked every door that he possibly could; before switching the television on. Edvard wanted there to be sufficient noise so that no-one could hear the discussions which took place. It was because Edvard had been part of the old system that he had come to trust no-one; he learned that trial by media was even worse than anything which he could have invented as Minister for Security, when he was still very much a red.
Robert spoke; though he wasn't entirely sure what he wanted from Mister Michalic.

"If I were to support you in forming government, what sort of position could I expect to be given in the next cabinet?"

Edvard considered the question carefully. His blue eyes, now safely protected by heavy spectacles, still gave away the fact that brain which they were stationed in front of, whirred at many thousands of revolutions per second.

"Do not expect to take the premiership. Neither should you expect the position of Chief Exchequer; for obvious reasons. Also do not expect to be the Minister for Defence, as we like to reserve that portfolio for someone who has come out of the armed services.

Maybe you could expect to be Minister for Health or the Minister for Environment and Land Care."

Robert thought for a second. The portfolios of Health, Justice and Education whilst vitally important, were all on a hiding to nothing. Being Health Minister meant that you were fighting the union of nurses constantly. Being Justice Minister meant that you were fighting the union of police constantly. Being Education Minister meant that you were fighting the union of teachers constantly and they were the most militant of all. Robert pressed him further about the portfolios of Trade, Foreign Relations and Industry but Edvard remained unmoved. He also threw in the unpalatable condition that Robert might have to join the KDP if he was going to become acceptable to the Party.

The meeting ended cordially and Robert took his leave. He went back to his office, not really having achieved very much but at least he knew that the KDP's number two was in principle, willing to offer him some sort of position in the cabinet; that was something.

Monday, 10th Mai, 1000.
In the afternoon, after wandering around town aimlessly, Robert returned to the office and considered his meeting with Anwar Ul-Huq.

He didn't really know much about Mister Ul-Huq because no-one really did. It is the fate of the opposition to be largely anonymous because they do not capture the public imagination.

The government gets to make policy announcements and are the ones responsible for the business of running the country but it is the lot of oppositions to mainly be the party of 'no'. Unless you are a particularly aggressive leader of the opposition, most of the time the press doesn't even care about you. Attacking the government is something which newspapers, television and radio does very well and since the press already has people writing copy which already does that, they have very little need of the opposition.

Arriving in Mister Ul-Huq's office, Robert was greeted by an advisor who promptly headed to the outer office and closed the door behind him. Anwar arrived from the central room and immediately Robert was struck at the size of the man standing before him. Anwar Ul-Huq stood six feet eleven inches tall and was solidly built. He was the sort of man whom you didn't want to meet in a dark alley; not because of what he might do to you but because he occupied so much space, that your progress down the alley would be impeded.

Anwar Ul-Huq was a man who admired aspiration and if he saw it within members of his own party, he gently pushed them towards greater roles. Although he had been nominated for the position of leader of the United Labour Party, he had always refused the nomination. He didn't even want the top job for himself but very much wanted to be the Chief Exchequer, for he had worked for a merchant bank and thought that his particular expertise would benefit the nation greatly.

He appeared to take interest in Robert's questions but Robert wondered what was really going on behind those dark brown eyes.

"Suppose for a minute that I were to support you on matters of supply. What sort of cabinet position would your party be willing to offer in return?"

"Initially, nothing. Then as the situation becomes more desperate, we might offer you either of the Health or Education portfolios."

Robert had been down this road only that morning. Presumably because the situation for both parties was roughly alike, so the solutions to the dilemma would also be roughly alike.

As before, being given the portfolios of Health and Education was kind of like being given a box of salmon – in theory it sounded like it might be a good idea but the longer the time period that you had to think about it, the more you realised that it stinks.

"How about Finance or Industry?"
"No."
"Why not?"
"We have a balancing game to play already. Our coalition with the Robots as you might well imagine, is like building a bridge from tissue paper and is based on many delicate assumptions, including that they be given key roles in government. At federal level it isn't really much of a problem but at provincial level it is fraught with seventeen kinds of difficulty.
In the province of Saint Nikola they outnumber us and in Woss Plotchka they hold government in their own right; we're not even in coalition with them."
"Surely those are provincial issues then?"
"Ha ha ha , no. Unless we negotiate with the Robots, there might not even be a coalition to consider. They might jump across to join the KDP; if that happens, then this discussion is as pointless as trying to pin a snowflake to the floor with a stake."
"Should I go and speak to the Robots as well then?"
"I you think you can, maybe you can try. I would think it a fruitless task. The Robots do not list a leader at federal level and when in government, they attend caucus meetings and cabinet meetings sporadically. They are like zebras. Yes, you might be able to catch one and they all are different but how would you know that you have the one you want?"

Robert thought about this for a moment and took a pause before he spoke again.

"Suppose that I were to become a member of the United Labour Party. What sort of cabinet position would you offer me in exchange for making that sort of commitment?"
"Initially, nothing. Then as the situation becomes more desperate, we might offer you…"
"Health and Education," they said in unison.

A phone call came from the outer room and Anwar apologised that the meeting had to be cut short. Robert had established that the stakes were practically identical no matter which side he supported and although this was an answer, it was unhelpful. He probably could negotiate his way into a cabinet position on either side (albeit one which wouldn't be 'fun') and in the end he would still have stable government. Did it really matter in the end which way he should go?

The people of his own constituency had marginally voted in favour of the KDP on first preferences but with less than one third endorsement, that still implied two-thirds disapproval. Even if he were to take a survey of all the members of parliament, there would still be sixty-two on one side and sixty-two on the other.

Minority governments had worked in other countries with some degrees of success. There were those countries that had rainbow coalitions on the floors of houses which meant that the term "hung parliament" didn't really mean very much but when there were two largely defined blocks, it mattered greatly.

Government mattered only for issues of confidence and supply. The problem with the current situation was that the two groups were equal in number and a speaker of the house had to be selected, which would again ensure that they were equal.

What did protocol demand? Mostly it ensured that the old government would still handle the affairs of the nation as caretakers until the King appointed a new government. This did not mean though that Robert was required to support the existing government. If parliament was ordered to sit, it could suffer an immediate loss of confidence and the nation would be off to the polls again.

At this point Robert decided, there might be only two opinions that really mattered in the whole country – his and Katherine's. If he made any decision, not only would he have to live with it for three years but he would have to hear from Katherine for three years if he had got it wrong.

Monday, 10th Mai, 1000.
Monday traffic on the way home was usually nonsensical but today proved to be a special kind of nonsense.

The A3 passed over a steel arch bridge which crossed a river valley way below. On the other side of the bridge, the A3 split into the A3 and the A31 but one lane was specifically reserved for buses. Cars that were in the outside lanes and who didn't want to continue along at A3, had to cross through the bus lane if they wanted to reach the exit for the A31.

On most days this was a slow and poorly orchestrated symphony but this afternoon, someone in a bright green sports car decided that they wanted to pass in front of a bus at more than 100km/h and had failed. Their previously hideously coloured shiny green sports car was now a hideously coloured shiny green pile of twisted metal.

Robert who hadn't been moving at all, heard over the radio that there was an accident ahead of him and so he phoned Katherine.

"I think that I'm going to be late getting home. Apparently there's some sort of accident ahead of me."
"I know."
"You know?"
"Yeah. I can actually see your face on television. Your little blue car is behind that white estate car."
"Really?"
"Wave. Come on wave at me?"
"Where am I waving?"

Robert waved his arms about and Katherine worked out where the camera was. She relayed the information about the accident ahead of him.

"You're going to be there for a long while as they cut the roof off to get the driver out. The car looks pretty mangled. It's a good thing that you're okay though."
"Yeah. Thanks."
"Oh, can you do one thing for me on the way home?"
"Sure, what is it?"
"We need eggs and bread and milk and silver cachous and…"
"Silver cachous? Are you making a cake?"
"No. I just want to hear the story of how the supermarket cashier looked when you buy all of these things."

When the phone call ended, Robert found that he had both the space and the time to think about what both Edvard Michalic and Anwar Ul-Huq had said. If neither party could offer him anything in return for his support, then why should he support either of them? He could just as easily go to the king and ask for a fresh election; though if he did that, what good would that do either?

He didn't know if it was an equation with no answer or with many answers. Politics wasn't like mathematics. With mathematics, there were laws and rules to follow to make sure that you got to the right answer and solved your problems. With politics, people either didn't know what the right answer war or deliberately put things in your way to give you more problems. He also thought about the problem of his own ego. So what if they made him Minister for Health or Education? What would be so bad about that? The work might be difficult but he'd have a whole department behind him and besides that, he'd be a Minister of the Crown. That in itself was a prize which he never expected to have. He hadn't even expected to be elected in the first place.

Monday, 10th Mai, 1000.
Katherine was far less concerned about protocol that Robert was. Katherine had previously worked in a primary school teaching third grade students and as far as she was concerned, there was no difference between eight and nine year old children and people in offices who wore suits and still carried on like children.

"Why don't you just shoot for the moon and just demand to be Prime Minister?" said Katherine, completely ambivalent to the consequences.

"What? You don't think…"

"I don't think anything. They need your vote to form government; you don't need anything from them at all. Why should you cower and kowtow to someone just because they happen to like having a fancy title. If you give either of them your support, you give them the biggest prize in politics, the Prime Ministership. Why not take that away from both of them and see just how much they're prepared to grovel for it?"

Robert was stunned by this notion. It was like being placed into check and then by moving just one pawn, claiming a checkmate of your own. There was a kind of refuge in audacity and the thought excited him. His eyes danced. Katherine's spark would be a raging fire which had the potential to burn down everyone's carefully constructed house of cards. Robert felt that he owed no one anything; so it really didn't matter. Even his election to the Commune Assembly was almost a complete fluke and so he literally had nothing to lose.

Robert went to bed and slept soundly that night. It was the sleep of the angels; such a beautiful dream.

Tuesday, 11th Mai, 1000.

The press were waiting for Robert as he exited his apartment block and a small army of reporters with microphones pressed him to divulge his intentions. He brushed aside their incessant questions with a stream of repeated "No comment". Even as he drove down the M3, he was aware that he was being shadowed by a press motorcade, which didn't particularly make the morning any easier.

His only respite in the morning was the short drive from the security boom gates to the car park. He knew that as soon as he would emerge from the elevators and walk through the parliamentary building that he would be followed again and so he resigned himself to this fact.

Inside The Shortcake, the press scrum only grew larger and rather than scurrying through the inner courtyards and corridors, Robert decided to enter through the public galleries and via the outer corridors to the offices. When he arrived at office 615, he paused to address the brood of vultures with their waiting microphones and cameras.

"Good Morning everyone, I have not yet decided as to whom I shall support in this term of parliament. I will hopefully make an announcement at four-forty-five this afternoon. Unless there is an official announcement from either Mister Brewin or Mister Diakonos before this time, do not expect any sort of statement from me regarding who I will support. Thank you and good morning."

Robert kept the door to his outer office open and sat down at his desk in full view of the press. Some of them pushed into his office, thinking that this was an invitation of some sort but Robert said nothing. He printed out an email from his local newspaper, the Astari Astra, pulled out a notepad from his desk drawer and proceeded to compose his thoughts, responding to their request to interview him.

Initially some members of the press were confused by this and although someone tried to ask him a question, he merely raised his finger and pressed it to his lips; telling them to "shh". After about fifteen minutes, they were all gone and Robert waiting for the last of them to be out of sight, closed the door behind them and retreated to his inner office, where he telephoned both Petr Brewin and Anton Diakonos; requesting an audience with both of them. They both naturally acquiesced.

Robert wrote down his very short list of demands, which only included that he be made Prime Minister of any government which would be formed and whichever of them agreed to it, would become his Deputy. He copied out his very short list of demands and taking both copies, sealed them both in cream envelopes bearing the franking mark "On His Majesty's Service", which he thought looked quite official.

Tuesday, 11th Mai, 1000.
Anton Diakonos was very keen for the meeting to occur and arrived five minutes early. Anton was so keen that he had even worn his best one-hundred-thousand Lek suit. He knocked firmly five times and waited at the door.

The door to the hallway of Robert's inner reception room had been left open. Robert remained in his office, between the two reception rooms but both doors were locked. This was to give the impression to the other Members of the House that the offices were empty; Anton Diakonos had learnt this little trick as a backbencher more than a decade and a half ago and had told Robert about it on the telephone.

Robert and Anton deliberately kept quiet, for they knew that the press might be outside in the public hallway and various members of parliament might accidentally walk past the office.

Robert took his very short list of demands and slid them across the table to Anton. Anton carefully prized open the envelope and took out the single piece of paper. He looked it up and down and was both surprised and secretly amused at the utter audacity shown by Robert but his outer countenance revealed nothing but scorn.

"You do realise that you cannot simple hold the government to ransom like this?" said Anton pushing back the clean white sheet of paper back across the table.
"Which government might that be?"
"My government." Anton slapped his hand on the table with all the aplomb and fury that one could muster after a decade as a proper statesman.
"I was led to believe that there was currently no government."
"You do know how this parliament works, don't you?" charged Anton.

Robert folded his hands in front of him as though he was addressing a select committee. He leaned forward slightly.
"'Government' is formed from a majority of members of the floor of the Commune Assembly," said Robert, quoting from his 500 Lek copy of the Constitution which he had bought on his very first day as a Member of Parliament. He paused as he tried to rein in his thoughts. "The KDP currently has sixty-two members who will side with them. You need sixty-three to form government. Without sixty-three, there is no majority; you have no government."

Anton was livid.
"You can't just waltz in here and demand to be the Prime Minister! There are rules and protocols and traditions that need to be followed."

"Indeed," said Robert. He slid open the top drawer of this desk and pulled out that very copy of his 500 Lek Constitution. It was a small purple book which tourists often bought and often forgot once they returned home again. He slid the sorry looking thing across the table.
"Go on. Find for me where it even mentions the post of Prime Minister."

Robert folded his arms. It was as though he had played a wrong-footed bishop one space, on a long diagonal that no-one could have seen and created a crafty check mate.

Anton blinked. He had joined the Communist Party at the age of seventeen; he had joined the KDP; he had waited his turn; he had fought his way up through the rank and file of the party; and now sitting across the table from him was an independent who had been a member of parliament for less than a fortnight and now demanding the very job which he had held for six years; and on top of that, he was doing so on the strength of the highest law in the land, the very Constitution itself.

The situation was impossible.

Anton sighed.

"You know that I cannot possibly accept this?"

"That's fine... I hope that you don't mind being the new leader of His Majesty's Most Loyal Opposition next week."

"What?"

"There really isn't anything more to say. You have been in these offices for some time now. I'm sure you'll find your way out."

"Why you little!"

"Please."

Robert stood up and bowed. Anton also stood up. He thought that if he stared long and hard into Robert's face that Robert would flinch but Robert closed his eyes and motioned towards the door as though it were a toaster on a game show.

Anton bowed and stepped towards the door. It dawned on him that if he were seen to be leaving Robert's office with a pleased expression on his face, that people might get the wrong impression. Half of the game of politics was making sure that you were seen to be doing something even if it was perfectly obvious to all that nothing had been done.

He sighed deliberately in an attempt to paint a worried expression on his face but he needn't have bothered. No-one was in the inner corridor and no-one would expect that a jumped up novice would demand one of the highest positions in the land.

Anton Diakonos, who still held the title of Prime Minister for the moment, until such time as a new government was formed, stepped quietly into the corridor to the ovation of no-one and thought to himself that the sound of silence was one of the greatest noises in the world.

Robert leaned on the lintel of his door and watched as Anton walked away from him, down the corridor. He knew that he would have to go through the whole process again. If Mister Brewin also thought that the idea was unacceptable, then what? He would have to answer that question later.

Tuesday, 11th Mai, 1000.
On the Monopoly board of offices, Petr Brewin's was 'Go to Jail' on the fifth floor. All of the corner offices were significantly larger than those down the sides; being as wide as they were deep. They also all ended with the number 1. Petr Brewin's office was particularly opulent as he had it fitted out with wooden panelling, frosted art-deco glass light fittings and extra thick plush pile carpeting.
Robert was led into an inner sanctum where a faded portrait of Comrade Gregor watched over a room with burgundy leather lounge suites, a floor standing globe drinks cabinet on wheels and where the ancient fug of cigar smoke still lived on as a ghost. It was as though you could smell history itself.

Robert took a seat, still clutching his "On His Majesty's Service" envelope with his very short list of demands inside. Petr, whose experience would by itself fill a series of novels, spied the envelope and correctly guessed its contents.

"May I?"
Robert handed over the envelope.
Petr slid a letter opener inside and ran it between the flap and the envelope; being careful not to tear the crisp paper.

"Ah yes. A brilliant list of demands, I must say," said Petr. "A list of demands which given the circumstances are understandably natural."
Robert smiled.

"But idiotic."

Those words cut through Robert like an oxy-acetylene torch carving through a pat of lard.

"This list says: 'Hand over the keys of the kingdom, or else it shall remain locked.'
Very smart; very brave; very stupid.
Do you honestly think that I could ever accept such a list of demands? Even if I did, it would have to be approved by the caucus and even if they approved it. It would have to further be approved by the Robots as well.
I must commend you on your attempt but it fails, even before it has arrived at the first hurdle."

Robert grew sad. He wasn't sure what he wanted to say at this point. Petr, noticing this, smiled; his wizened eyes danced and flickered. It was this kind of charm which had helped him to rise through the ranks of the United Labour Party. It was also his ruthlessness which kept him in at the top of the tree.

"Can I be so bold as to leave you with a question? What do you want this parliament to do for you? When you decide what you want, then we shall see what sort of concessions we are both willing to make and how we are to achieve those ends, whatever they may be.
Going all in when there are no cards on the table will not win you a pot of gold. People will fold instantly and ask to play the next hand."

The rest of the meeting was not about politics, nor did any further negotiations take place. Mainly it was about Petr regaling a new person who had not previously heard his ramblings, with tales of past glories and days of yore. Robert spoke little. Eventually Robert took his leave and was quietly glad to be out of there.

He did not notice the band of meerkats staring at him as he walked back to his office. He also did not notice as Albert Andriyv, followed him along the last side of the board and back to his office. He was startled when Albert knocked on the door behind him.

Mister Andriyv addressed Robert with a stream of invective that would have made a sailor blush, had Plotchka had a navy, which it didn't. Mister Andriyv made it very clear that he had his own list of demands.

Specifically, he demanded to know why he hadn't been consulted as head of the Socialist Robot Party about who Robert would support on the floor. Robert explained that in the official telephone directory, the Socialist Robots hadn't actually listed who was head of the party.

Albert apologised profusely and sheepishly. He knew full well that the reason that the Socialist Robots hadn't listed a party leader was to symbolically emphasise the equality of all members of the party but he didn't mention this to Robert. He bowed and took his leave, leaving Robert standing and leaning against the lintel of his doorway, both feeling confused and slighted.

Tuesday, 11th Mai, 1000.
At three minutes past five in the afternoon, after Robert had locked the door to his offices and was walking through the public gallery, he noticed Petr Brewin speaking quite crossly to someone on the telephone. He didn't think very much of it until he heard one phrase in particular: "that Ilanyich chap." He continued to listen, by remaining inconspicuous and looking down at his own mobile telephone.

"How come I wasn't told about him beforehand? Find out who he is, the absolute cheapest price that he will accept and how easily he can be bought off.
…
He has to have come from somewhere. Is he a KDP plant? Is he an operative for The Globe or some other media company? I want to know, who paid for his registration as a candidate, who he's supported in the rest of his political career and how we can bend him to join us. I don't care what you have to do either. Go through his bins for all I care. I'll expect to hear from you in the morning."

Petr ended the phone call and exited through the main entrance; Robert did not know what to think. Did the political parties have some form of clandestine operation, left over from when the country was still communist, working for them? It was cause for concern and weighed very heavily on his mind as he drove home.

As he drove home, the sky turned black and an eerie sleet began to fall. With a wall of darkness in front of him and the red glow of the sunset in the rear view mirror, he felt uneasy and pensive. In the outside lane, there were still mad people doing more than 200km/h despite the slush now forming on the road surface. Although this was Mai, Plotchka's official summer would not begin for another twenty days; even then summer was a sort of misnomer.

The average high temperature in summer was only twenty-seven degrees Celsius, whilst in winter, minus six was normal. The absolute coldest day had occurred when Robert was a small boy and 'the great freeze' of 967, saw a daytime temperature of minus fourteen and a night-time chill of minus thirty-three. Snow in Juli wasn't impossible although uncommon but sleet could arrive on any day of the year that it felt like.

When Robert did make his way off the M3 and into Astari, the sleet had turned to slush and then refrozen, leaving small plates of ice on the road surface. This was particularly dangerous as braking distances were vastly increased and skidding and skating was so much of a hazard that the possibility of rear end crashes was very real indeed.

Robert decided to park the car on a side street for fear of something accidentally sliding into it at less than walking speed. It was a lesson that he had learnt with his first car; one that he did not wish to repeat.

Chapter 6.
"Fools are headstrong and do what they like; wise people take advice"

Wednesday, 12th Mai, 1000.

Some time ago, Robert had worked out that they best way to deal with the press was to hide in plain sight. He found that if he diverted his office phone to his mobile and worked in the public galleries, reporters tended to lose interest. This morning though, he was sitting out on the steps of The Shortcake and staring down The Boulevard Of The Heroes, otherwise known as the A5.

It was a monstrous ten lane ribbon stretching to the horizon with five virtually empty lanes in each direction. On the median strip were bronze statues of soldiers and scientists, veterans and victims as well as Marx and Lenin just for good measure.

At the very edge of visibility was the blue onion dome which sat atop Karl-Marx Metro Station. Robert thought that it was amusing that the great statue of the bearded gentleman, faced away from it as if to say "oh dear, what have I done?"

The five chimney stacks of the old Grimwelt Ironopolis peeked over red tiled terrace houses as if some steamship was in port. The stacks remained dormant and lifeless for twenty years and plans were afoot to gut the buildings and repurpose them as office space and chic new apartments.

The starkest thing out here was that the signs of progress were decrepitly obvious. Building work was going on all over the city but never completed. What wasn't as obvious though, was where any of the money came from to start such projects or even pay for it all. As far as anyone could see, the gears of industry had long since rusted and jammed and apart from a few legacy industries, it wasn't immediately obvious who if anyone, was doing any real work at all. Apart from copper and tin mining in Eoss Plotchka, what did the Plotchkan economy stand on?

It was some time after ten o'clock that Robert noticed four black sedans coming down the boulevard. The Winter Palace was in the northwest of the city and so the natural assumption was that the king himself must have been on the move. It was then that Robert remembered some obscure clauses in the constitution, so he closed his laptop and headed back inside The Shortcake.

The Government was required by the constitution to send a member of the executive for an audience with the king on a regular basis, to advice the king on government business. In practice, this meant weekly and usually the Prime Minister of the day went. Seeing as the position of the Prime Minister wasn't specifically named in the constitution, it meant that occasionally other cabinet ministers would go, such as the Chief Exchequer or the Minister of Defence if the need arose.
At least for the moment, there was no formal government; so this gave Robert an idea.

He strode purposefully into the Office of Parliament and Protocol. If there was no formal government and his was the casting vote which determined the outcome one way or the other, then logically the entire business of government for the moment effectively rested upon his shoulders. If government business depended on his decision, then also logically, he should be able to ask for that audience with the king.
He stepped up to the reception desk and asked for some advice upon the issue and was politely asked to take a seat and wait. Unbeknownst to him, the Office of Parliament and Protocol took his request most seriously indeed and after a short period, he was greeted by a man dressed in ermine and silver chains.

"Good Morning and welcome to you.
My name is Mikhail Kubasov and I am The Doorkeeper of the Last Watch. I am informed that you are Robert Ilanyich, Member for Astari and you seek an audience with the king, for advice and guidance on the matter of the currently hung parliament."
"Th-th-that's right," spluttered Robert.

The Doorkeeper of the Last Watch was one of the oldest of all the parliamentary officers. It was The Doorkeeper's job of officially close the walls of the Niuw General Platz if it was under attack. It was also The Doorkeeper's job to officially close the doors to the Commune Assembly and the Senate whilst it was sitting to ensure that the King (or formerly the President when the communists were in power did not enter the chamber. He was the keeper of two iron rods which barred the gates of the Niuw General Platz and the chambers of the two houses. Upon entering the chambers of parliament, these rods were placed on the floor in front of the doors and so the members who entered the chambers had to symbolically cross over them. If the king entered the chambers to open a sitting of parliament, he even required express written permission from The Doorkeeper of the Last Watch.

"We have considered your request and think that it is not only appropriate and correct that you should seek the advice of the king with respect to the current state of the parliament but we think that your request is quite worthy of this office to grant. Call forth the purser."

Echoes calling forth the purser could be heard down an out of sight hall way and from behind a door, the purser appeared; bearing a small wooden box. Inside the wooden box was a silver key, which was about eight inches long, which also symbolically opened the lock to the gates of the Niuw General Platz. It was as if Robert was being told by a doting father "These are the keys. Why don't you drive for a while?"

Robert accepted the key but that wasn't the end of it. Before he would even be accepted into the palace, he required further permission and so, according to practice, he signed off on the official letter which would go before him and request his entry. The letter once signed and sealed in a yellow envelope, was sent by parliamentary courier to the palace and Robert was directed to a waiting room deep in the bowels of The Shortcake where an armoured car would eventually be waiting for him. He didn't have to wait long though. The palace was just as keen to have the issue of government resolved as anyone else did and so they accepted the request without question.

It was one of the strangest trips that Robert had ever been on, in his whole life. The car left via a security exit and he could barely see out of the heavily tinted windows. Robert was bundled into a bullet-proof limousine after being frisked for weapons and one of the Royal Guards sat in the back seat with him.

Naturally when the car left The Shortcake, it aroused excitement. Speculation abounded and telephone calls were made to various media outlets. The ship of state is the only ship which leaks from the top, and on this particular day, no attempts were being made to bail it out.

They would not hesitate to kill if they thought that they need arose.

Robert thought of the days of his youth and wondered if this was how the secret service made unpersons of people that they did not like.

The media who by this stage were desperate to report anything, had sent out news vans to follow the black limousine and Robert began to feel the biggest sense of aloneness that he had ever felt in his life. Channel 12 had even decided to send up a helicopter to train cameras from the sky, down on proceedings; hoping to pick up anything that they could find. Either fortunately or unfortunately, the windows were tinted with such a dark tint, that no-one from the outside could see it.

The limousine made its way across St Matthews Bridge to the Ile du Plotchka, through the gatehouse and up the road which led to the palace; where it disappeared to an underground car park. No media outlets could see from here - not Channel 12's helicopter, not the Channel 8's "First at Five" news van and not even the resources of Plotchka Radio 1. The world would have to wait for now.

Instead of arriving through the front gates of the palace, the car drove in through a heavily guarded side entrance where the guards carried loaded rifles.

Robert was directed to a very large waiting room with marbled floors; which was overly cold and draught and was told to sit; a request with which he duly complied. He felt nervous and very afraid. The feeling was worse than when he had gotten into trouble and was made to sit outside of the principal's office in high school.

The king had more than just the power to expel someone from school, he had the power to execute them.

Wednesday, 12th Mai, 1000.
When an attendant of the king's household found a yellow envelope from a member of the Commune Assembly, he thought that it would finally be a letter advising that some arrangement had been reached and that a new government would be formed quickly. He opened the letter expecting to see either the handwriting of Anton Diakonos which he had seen many times before, or possibly Petr Brewin, who he would expect to see as the next Prime Minister if a change of government had taken place.

Opening the letter with his silver letter opener, he was taken aback to see that this letter was from neither of those two great men but instead was from someone he had never even heard of before. Robert Ilanyich, was the newly appointed Member for Astari in the province of Eoss Plotchka, which was distinctly working class. The attendant thought that the letter was some sort of strange joke.

Reading further, it appeared that this Mister Ilanyich, was requesting an audience with the king under the terms which would usually be reserved for the Prime Minister but seeing as no formal government had yet been established, nor this letter advise that one would be formed as yet, it appeared as though this man was asking for advice.

The letter was rushed through the palace as quickly as possible.

The king's personal secretary Martyn read the letter and handed it to King Josep.

"What do you make of this, sire?"

"I make very little of it. There are either two options here. Either this fellow is a madman or he is genuinely seeking advice."

"What shall we do, sire?"

"Martyn, this is not at all difficult. Bring this Mister Ilanyich, to us according to his request. He shall undergo all of the necessary security checks and if he passes, I can see no reason why he should not be granted an audience, if that is in fact all he wishes."

"But sir?"

"Martyn, if this fellow is a madman, he shall be shot before he ever even reaches this chamber. The Royal Guard will say that this was done in the defence of the realm and that this was a regicide attempt which was thwarted. If this fellow is genuine, then we shall have tea with him and we shall hear what he has to say.

We shall grant his request. Have Mister Ilanyich brought here for the audience he desires."

After being searched for a second occasion, having palace security investigate places which were demeaning, Robert was led through the palace; down a hallway with all of the doors closed and was asked to sit on a chair outside the king's personal office. A sentry sat with him.

He remembered back to his days of school and waiting outside the principal's office after he had been caught down at a local creek, skiving off school for the day. This was kind of like that, except that he was in sight of four armed guards.

An attendant from inside the kings' chamber stepped into the hallway.

"Halt! Who comes there?" said the attendant.

The sentry sitting next to Robert stood up and with arms by his sides announced "The Keys."

"Whose keys?"

"King Josep's keys," said the sentry.

They both stared at Robert expectantly. He suddenly remembered the silver key in his pocket, pulled it out and held it in front of him.

"Pass, King Josep's keys. All is well," said the attendant who walked back to the door of the king's chamber. Robert assumed that he should just go ahead and open the door; so he put the key into the lock and turned it. On the other side of the door, the king's personal secretary Martyn opened the door and bade him enter.

Robert was surprised to see what he found. The king's personal office contained a banker's desk with a lamp; with two chairs opposite, a leather lounge chair, a television screen, a fridge and a kettle, two filing cabinets and wall length bookcase with cabinets below. For a position so important, the décor seemed so mundane.

The guard whispered something in the king's ear, to which he nodded and motioned them to leave. The king also informed Martyn that his presence would not be required and that he should close the door behind him as he left.

The locks clicked the door closed quietly. King Josep V could see the look of terror which now swept across the face of the Federal Member for Astari, Robert Ilanyich, who was now seated in front of him on the other side of the table. He smiled. Robert thought the worst as the king slid open a lower drawer in his desk but he needn't have worried, for the king produced a bottle of Eduardo's Yellow Label Whiskey. He poured two glasses and Robert's mind clicked as he wondered about the value of the drink now sitting in front of him, as this 25 year old whiskey was worth well over forty-thousand Lek a bottle.

The king spoke.

"Robert... Robert Ilanyich is it?"
"Yes... yes... your majesty."
"No no no no no no no..." the king waggled his finger, "This will not do. The door is closed. This room is not bugged. No cameras can see in here. In this room, I am just Josep. Call me Jo."
"Thank you... your maj... Jo."

The king nudged one of the glasses of whiskey.

"Take a sip. It's nice. I assure you, there's nothing amiss with it. It is safe. In fact, this is probably the safest room in the whole kingdom."

Robert took a sip of the brown liquid. It was stunning. A quarter of a century of American White Oak had infused its way into its being. It was like the taste of a thousand summer camp fires, of nights spent with the violin and the guitar, of dancing, of a wedding in the village where everyone including people you'd never spoken to before arrived, of grand concerts, of cool afternoons in the garden and of the whole of Plotchka distilled. Robert smiled. The look of fear still shone through his eyes.

"Robert... I admire your audacity. To seek an audience with the king requires a great deal of courage. Courage is not the absence of fear, courage is looking fear in the face and doing it anyway. Now then... why did you seek an audience with me?"
"Sire... Jo... I am scared."
"You don't have to be scared in here Robert."
"No, Jo..." Robert stomped down the fear inside of him. The act of calling the king 'Jo' helped to dissolve his worries. "Jo... I have a choice and I'm horribly inadequately equipped to deal with it."
"Ah."
"As it stands, there are two sides to this parliament; both with sixty-two members. I alone hold both the balance of power and I alone currently have the power to be the 'kingmaker' as it were."
"Yes. I can see how that would be an issue."
"I chose to seek your advice because I never really expected to even be a member of parliament. The parliament has the power to make laws for the peace, order, and good government of the nation and I'm worried about making a decision in the spirit of 'good government'."

King Josep V stood up. King Josep V walked around the desk. Robert froze. King Josep V wrapped his arms around Robert and squeezed him tightly before slapping both of his arms and smiling.

"Robert Ilanyich, Member for Astari, did you know that in twenty-four years, since the restoration of this kingdom and the inception of the constitution, I have had nine Prime Ministers sit in the very chair which you now occupy and not one of them ever mentioned 'good government' as a motivation for policy?"
"Can I confess to something?"
"Sure. You can say anything in here.""

Robert looked downwards. He was suddenly ashamed of his acts of bravado which had brought both him and indeed the parliament to this point.

"I kind of caused this problem."
"How?"
"In trying to negotiate who I would lend my support to, to form the new government, I demanded that I be the next prime minister... to both sides."
"Politics is a messy messy game, Robert." The king went over to his leather couch and sat down, he patted the couch with his left hand an indicated for Robert to sit next to him. Picking up the remote control, he turned the television on to Channel 5A which was running a block of rolling news until any information came to hand. The king spoke again.

"Do you see this? Mostly the news is rubbish. Most of what the news reports is nothing more than speculation, claim, counter-claim and counter-counter-claim. The art of Politics is always about looking at what chips you have to play with and then playing accordingly."
"So what do I do then?"
"What do you 'do'? What do you 'do'?! Why what you do right now, is accept my offer that you join me for lunch; that we turn the television off; that you let the nation worry itself into a stupor for a little while longer, and that you make your decision in all the space and time that you need."
"Will you join me Robert?"
"Yes Jo."
"Remember, out there, I'm 'Your Majesty' again."
"Yes Jo."

King Josep V and Robert Ilanyich, Member for Astari, left the king's personal office and closed the door behind them. The king's personal secretary Martyn, stood outside; looking worried and at a moment's notice was prepared to have Robert shot.

"Sire. Is this fellow a madman?"
"No Martyn, Robert Ilanyich is not a madman. He is possibly the most sane member of His Majesty's Government."
"Sire. There currently is no government"

"Oh Martyn, Martyn, Martyn... young Robert's casting vote of support will create a government. This parliament is poised on a knife edge. Unless you know something that we do not, it is currently impossible for Robert to become a member of the Loyal Opposition."

Wednesday, 12th Mai, 1000.

Channel 5A who had kept one of their outside broadcast vans directly outside the Winter Palace had been waiting on any small morsel of information so that they might be first with any news on the impending government formation. When a 'source close to the Prime Minister' had secretly passed on the information that the black limousine did not contain Anton Diakonos, the news service went into overdrive. Both Channel 8 and Channel 12 who were watching the watcher, had noticed that one of the Channel 5A reporters was doing a piece to camera; this virtually caused a paroxysm of hysteria.

Channel 12 put its helicopter into the air and although there was a no-fly zone directly over the Winter Palace, the pilot and camera operators did their best to see if they could get any view of inside the palace.

Back at The Shortcake, various members of the press were roaming the halls; asking anyone for any kind of idea of who might be visiting the king; when they asked The Doorkeeper of the Last Watch, they got stony silence. Proper protocol was in place and security procedures demanded that no-one was ever told who had left to see the king.

Inside the Winter Palace, King Josep V, king's personal secretary Martyn, twelve year old Princess Eleanor and Robert Ilanyich, were sitting at a table with a green worsted baize top; playing Contract Bridge.

The king thought that given enough time, the press would finally lose interest in their little games and return to their normal reportage of things being blown up in the Middle East and the endless parade of celebrity and sports. Robert would be smuggled out of the palace by one of the palace's staff and deposited a few blocks away from The Shortcake. The press were almost always fooled by ennui and the mundane.

Wednesday, 12th Mai, 1000.

The long journey back from the Winter Palace was simultaneously deflating and frustrating. Robert knew that never again could he expect to be in the company of royalty and on top of that, he was still no closer to making his decision about who he would support to form government.

Did it really matter in the end though? The nation looked like it was doing perfectly fine without a formal government. He remembered that some nations had gone for weeks following a hung parliament without a formal government and from 996 to 997, Belgium went for a period of 589 days without an formal government. Belgium did perfectly fine in that period.

If he continued to do nothing, what would be the consequences of inactivity? In the unlikely event that the nation was invaded or dragged into some continental war, then more than likely a unity government would be formed and his decision would scarcely matter anyway. If those sorts of events were to take place, then even without a formal cabinet it didn't really matter because the King was the head of the armed forces anyway. In the year 900, events across Europe took a mere thirty-seven days to collapse from an uneasy peace to total war.

The only real consequence that was likely, that Robert could see, would be if a budget "failed to pass" the Senate. In this case because no government would exist to write the appropriation bills, then the budget would fail to pass because it would fail to exist. The budget was normally handed down in November for the following year starting Januar 1. If there was no budget within six months of that date, then the King could close down the parliament and call for fresh elections but those would not take place until Saturday the third of Juni, 1001; which was thirteen months away.

When Robert arrived back in his office, there were all sorts of requests to appear at schools and even an invitation to attend the opening of a local swimming pool. This gave Robert an idea. Why not just hold a public forum in the town hall and ask the members of his constituency, who had elected him, for their input. What were their pressing concerns and issues? Who did they ultimately want to govern the nation?

Robert phoned up his local council and asked to speak to someone so that he could hire the town hall for an evening. His phone call was passed from the reception desk, to a planning department, back to the reception desk and then back to the same person in the planning department who had passed him on before.

Organising the use of the town hall was deceptively easy. Apart from a folk dancing group which used the hall on Monday nights and the "world famous" lotto night on Fridays (where fabulous prizes such as pillow cases, tinned meats, cheap wine and one new car which still hadn't been won in nine years, could be won), the other nights of the week were free. Robert decided that if he could get the announcement to appear in the newspaper both tomorrow and one week hence, then it would make sense to book the town hall for Wednesday week.

As he was on the phone making arrangements, word had got around to the Mayor of Astari. Yeshua Guldblat, who had once been a relatively popular radio host and was elected to the position of Mayor of Astari in a landslide, was a virtuoso in self-promotion and self-aggrandisement. Naturally, he wanted in on the publicity and cut in on the phone call; offering both the town hall free of charge and himself as master of ceremonies. Robert agreed to this, if for no other reason that the event would be run properly.

Robert turned his attention to advertising the event. He phone the Astari Novosti newspaper and they were only too happy to accept the proposed propaganda. They also offered to run the notices for both weeks on page five for free; knowing that for them it meant a potential chance to break sales records and for some of the staff, a chance to get out of the Astari Novosti and work for a more prestigious newspaper - Astari was seen as a ten-Lek town with a population of five goats, four sheep and a dog named Daniil.

Chapter 7.
"Should your springs overflow in the streets, your streams of water in the public squares?"

Thursday, 13th Mai, 1000.
On the very bottom floor of The Shortcake, there was both a cafeteria and a 'members only' bar. By law the bar and lounge remained free of surveillance devices and convention decreed that anything said there, like the chambers of the parliament, fell into the realm of parliamentary privilege. Thus, no end of useful discussions, across party lines were held there throughout the years and although it might very well have been a form of collusion on a number of things, it also meant that a lot of difficult policy decisions were nutted and hacked out, far from the prying eyes and ears of the press.
Robert stumbled into the lounge one day, almost by accident when he was looking for an entrance to the underground car park. It was not mentioned in any official guide to parliament and he found the place virtually empty.
The only person apart from the staff member behind the bar was the Finance Minister, Tomas Doss.

Doss was a veteran of the parliament; having been there since 985. As he was now 63, he was marginally younger than Robert was now, when he had started. Prior to that, he had a colourful past, as one of the group of secret service agents which finally leaked all the documents which would finally bring down the communists.

Tomas called Robert over and motioned for him to sit down. Robert obliged but knew that any minute that he spent here, was a minute that would not be spent on the M3 and home.

"Are you one of us, or one of them?"
"I'm one of neither."
"Ah, so you're an Indy. There aren't many of you. What, are there five if you this time around?"
"Yes, sir."
"Oh well, one of you will eventually decide how this mess works itself out. Whatever the result is, I'm sure that we're going to have fun over the next three years."

Robert wasn't sure if Tomas' was just being jovial or whether the effects of excessive lubrication by fermented vegetable products had taken hold.

A gilt sign above the entrance door bore the words "The Shame Room" and it like the rest of the room was an idiosyncratic piece of detritus set against the seriousness of the affairs above. There were many bookcases with leather bound books; most of which were works of literature which had been banned when the communists were in power. Some were works of satire, others treatises on the operation of government and there were even a few copies of key legislation, which had been annotated and tagged.
Upstairs the world was organised into two rival camps which hated each other but down here, the rules of party and faction did not apply.

Tomas gradually twinged about who he was speaking to. He sprang into a state of alertness, if not outright alarm.

"You're that guy... the new guy who hasn't made up his mind yet."
"Yeah, I'm that guy."
"I'd better start being nice to you. You are the one who holds the crossed keys to heaven."
"I don't think I'm Saint Peter or anything."
"Maybe not but when you finally open the seventh seal, the trumpets will sound and we will find out if we find our way to heaven or the other place."
"Hell?"
"The Opposition front bench."

Thursday, 13th Mai, 1000.
If you drive the same piece of road, day in and day out, you build up an intimate knowledge of the journey's minutiae. Robert learned that the fastest lane for the majority of the run home was actually the second of four, and that if you wanted to make that exit off the M3 and back to Astari, then you had to move over well before the two kilometre board came into view because there were so many cars trying to funnel into one rather puny slip road.

He didn't realise before that the colour of bricks which were used to build public housing, changed like one colour being worked into the next one on a canvas. Even in just twenty years, the main shade of bricks had changed from the brown of ginger but biscuits, to that shade of brown which came to settle on television sets and record players in the 960s, when he was a boy.

His own apartment building, which was set in grey off-form concrete, used to have a name but only the letter Б was left; the rest of the brass letters having fallen off at some time in the long forgotten past.

Katherine was now home before Robert, every night of the week. Whereas he used to be able to get dinner started (and in some cases completely finished) by the time she got home, his commute now made that impossible. The upside was that in the time that she was home before him, she could turn up the stereo as loud as she wanted; that meant blaring songs from their childhood whilst music was still made by real people with real instruments. The irony with that though, was that thirty years ago, songs both railing against communism and pro-communist songs put out by the Politburo were popular. Did that imply a sense of irony or nostalgia?

Only a few days into the job, Robert rediscovered the joys of slow cooking and the nice aspect that you could switch the slow cooker on in the morning; before you even went to work. Katherine responded by raiding the recipe books of her grandmother and much to her surprise, the dishes though a little spartan, were for the most part quite delicious.

Columbine and Harlequin although having their interest piqued initially, soon gave up as the learned that the slow cooker was impregnably armoured.

Friday, 14th Mai, 1000.

When the mail arrived on Friday morning, Robert couldn't believe the amount of letters that he'd received from people from all over the country. Mostly they were from supporters who wanted him to consider their side to lead the country but still others were not very thinly veiled abuse. There was a feeling of weariness in the electorate almost a fortnight after the election and some people were beginning to blame politicians for not being able to do their supposed job.

Politics is always like this though. People like having someone to blame and a concept as vague as 'the government' has being the panacea to cure everything, the root cause of all evil and something which people either thought should have more or less control in people's lives, is what keeps many journalists and commentators in business.

After what felt like hours of answering people's mail, Robert was surprised to find Ivan Nilsson knocking at the door. He was becoming more impatient about the lack of government. Robert let him in and they sat in the middle room between the two offices.

"I've come here to offer you something of an olive branch."

"Oh."

"I've just been in a meeting with Anton Diakonos and he hinted at the possibility of giving me the portfolio of Infrastructure if I could convince you to join us."

"Well that's all very nice but what would be offered to me if that were to happen?"

"We hadn't discussed that."

"So what was your point in coming here?"

"The thing is, that if I could be given something like Infrastructure maybe they'd give you the Arts or Sport or something."

Robert thought about this. Ivan had wanted everyone to follow him days ago; now he was waiving about the possibility that he would be given a cabinet portfolio with no guarantee of anything else. It was weird that this was coming from Ivan and not either the Prime Minister or the Chief Exchequer. This was suspicious.

"To summarise," reasoned Robert; still not sure of where he was going, "you have already signed off on an agreement with the KDP and you come in here with an offer that isn't really an offer but a set of guesses and you expect me to jump when you say 'jump' and ask 'how high?' I don't understand."

"Look, none of us want to be hanging about in this state of knowing any longer than we have to. If the stack of mail that I got, and probably you got, was anything to go by, then the public doesn't like it either. The press sure as heck aren't going to leave you alone until you make up your mind.
You mark my words. Standing with your feet in two boats that are slowly drifting apart isn't going to end up very pretty.
You're going to end up in the water and looking very wet and silly."

Friday, 14th Mai, 1000.
Robert had a fairly boring kind of trip home. Traffic on the M3 was about as freely moving as could be expected and reasonably well behaved. The number of instances of truly selfish driving was minimal and everyone sort of accepted their usual fate of needing to move over well in advance for their exit. In fact, the only real difficulty was a surfeit of politeness at a four-way stop sign when no one was really sure who had the right of way at all and sat around in a state of confusion.
Robert stopped at a petrol station not too far from home and was filling the tank when his mobile phone buzzed in his back pocket. He pulled it out; expecting a message from Katherine asking what he would like for dinner but found five missed calls from her. He dutifully made a call.

"Hello? It's me. Is anything the matter?"

There was no reply but quiet sobbing on the other end of the line.

"I'll be there right away. I'm only at the petrol station on the main street."

He filled the remainder of the tank and drove like Fangio on the way home; almost collecting a bollard in the car park under their building, ran through the car park and then tore up the six flights of stairs to their apartment, rather than having to wait for the elevator which was installed before the advent of colour television.
He found Katherine sitting in a ball on the couch; with her eyes and face as red as yesterday's borscht.

"It was horrible," Katherine spluttered, "there were TV cameras here and I wouldn't let them in but there were too many and they barged their way in and then Harlequin was all hissing and growling and I told them to get out and then Columbine shot across the room and got out the door and now I don't know where she is."

Robert fumed. It was one thing for the media to harass him at work but quite another for them to invade his him and still even worse for them to cause one of his cats to run away.
They had found both Columbine and Harelquin as very small kittens, in a cardboard box under a motorway overpass; they had obviously been either abandoned, forgotten or orphaned by their mother and after taking them to the veterinarian to check to see if they were all right, they adopted them as their own. The two cats had never been a day apart before and being brother and sister, they liked each other very much; hence their names.
They had both been tagged and chipped but because they'd spent their whole lives living in apartment blocks, Katherine was sure that neither of them would fend very well in the big wide scary world.

Robert telephoned the local police station and the constable explained that if they were found and turned in, then it would be the located council who would be responsible for their return. Knowing what he did about the local council and their competency (only last year they had managed to accidentally connect the suburb's gas mains to the water supply, whilst making repairs to damage which they caused), he wasn't hopeful that they could find a way out of a wet paper bag with holes torn in it, much less a small brown cat with a predilection and talent for hiding in small spaces.

Robert went both downstairs and upstairs in the building, knocking on every door but there was either no answer or no one who had any knowledge of where Columbine might be. Robert finally abandoned his search and returned home, to collapse on the couch. Harlequin sat on the floor, staring at him, visibly enraged that his companion was gone and that people were at fault.

Saturday, 15th Mai, 1000.
Katherine had already left to play tennis by the time Robert woke from his inadequate state of nocturnal rest. Sleep had not come to stay and worry's two children of anxiety and doubt had played all night long in the fields of Robert's mind; leaving big brown divots in the grass.
Robert vacuumed the apartment, swept the kitchen floor and collected all of the laundry to take down to the laundromat. Harlequin had still not forgiven the world of people and sulked and hissed whenever Robert went near him.

"I'll find Columbine," said Robert weakly, "I'll find Columbine if it's the last thing I do."

With a sack of laundry slung over one shoulder, Robert was the most disappointing Saint Nicholas the world had ever seen. If the children wanted what came from his sack of goodies, they must have been quite daft, for unless there is some deranged child in the world who actually wants dirty laundry for Christmas, they would choose to be naughty. At least then they might be given some coal to keep the boiler going.

The walk to the laundromat was not terribly far. Businesses like this had sprung up all over the place during the 910s when people started moving to terrace houses and towers with no laundry of their own. Maybe the communists thought that the proletariat like to be the great unwashed masses.
At any rate, there were so many terrace houses and tower blocks that there would always be a substantial queue to use the washing machines: a strange irony since Robert had worked in the factory which made them.
Robert left his laundry bags on a conveyor belt which served as the queue, took a small beeper from the attendant and went next door to the coffee shop where he went every Saturday morning.

Everyone knew the routine. Robert entered the coffee shop, raised a hand so that the barista knew that he was there and took a seat at the back of the shop and a copy of The Globe, before settling down for some bristling conversation with no one. This is how it always was. Great novels like Antonov's "Dishonesty and Retribution" and Mäkkinen's epic "The Speed Of The Forest", were written in silence in coffee shops like this. They were all long rooms like single lane bowling alleys, with tables down the sides and not enough light to be comfortable, which was handy as it helped to hide the grime.

Robert was halfway reading through an article about Dysprosium which he didn't understand when there was a commotion at the door and three reporters showed up. Even the quiet enjoyment of Saturday morning had been destroyed.

"Can you tell us which way you are leaning at the moment?"
"What would sway you one way or the other?"
"Do you think that the public should have a say in your final decision?"

Questions came at him before he had a chance to answer any of them. He lifted his hands and they all stopped. Silence fell across the whole coffee shop and the proprietor even turned down the volume of the radio.

"People like you; maybe even you; I don't know because I wasn't at home, barged your way into my apartment last night. Their rudeness and hurry to get a story caused my cat to run away through the door behind them. My cat is currently missing. I don't come to your house and ask you why you can't seem to use proper grammar in your stories and I don't see why you should come to my house and pester me or my family about my job.
Not only am I not going to tell you who I'm going to support to form government but when I do formally make my announcement, it won't be to any of you brood of asps but to the editors of the New York Times and Joson Inmingun."

Robert smiled, looked down at his newspaper and carefully and deliberately turned the page as slowly as he could. When one of the trio tried to ask him another question, he raised one finger like the conductor of the orchestra giving a final flourish before the end of the movement.

They did not bother him anymore and left.

After normality had returned, Robert read on about more trouble brewing in Jerusalem, how the EU still couldn't come to an agreement during this round of discussions on agricultural policy and how Bobat Herschel had not turned up for training all week at Kynzil Locomotiv.

It didn't matter to him this morning that the country still did not have formal government: his cat Columbine was out there somewhere. The nation could take a flying leap off a short pier if they expected an answer today. The decision would not be made today.

Saturday, 15th Mai, 1000.

Lugging home a sack of laundry is usually not the most pleasurable experience at the best of times and this was only heightened by knowing that Columbine was missing. Robert started to see things that were cat-shaped but they turned out to be plastic bags, cardboard boxes and one deviant carpet square playing a game of masquerade.

He got back to the apartment, dumped everything on the bed and was crankily sorting out the clothes when Katherine came home.

"How was your morning?"
"Rubbish."
"Mine too."

A tacit agreement fell over the room. They had been married for so long that they both knew that it was best not to stir up trouble in situations like this and given that they both knew why the other was so grumpy, there was little more if anything that needed to be said.

Harlequin, who was still angry at the human race for kidnapping his sister, walked into the room because he couldn't stand to be alone and started yelling as best as a cat can. Upon seeing that he was being ignored he jumped into the pile of unsorted clothes and meowed as though pleading that they make it all better.

"I've had enough of this. I'm going to look for that cat," declared Robert.
"You do that. It'll help both of us."

Robert left the bedroom and the apartment and the building. Katherine could only watch from the balcony, as he turned from being a small person, to a white maggoty blob; before disappearing out of sight.

Saturday, 15th Mai, 1000.
Katherine sulked, Robert wandered, Harlequin took guard by the door and waited; the nation carried on as normal.
After almost four hours, Robert abandoned his search as futile. Columbine where ever she was, was not going to be found. Miserably he turned his attention to writing emails and imagining questions that would be thrown at him on Wednesday night at the Town Hall. That also seemed futile now.

Katherine suggested that Robert stand in front of a mirror and practice posing, pointing and looking thoughtful; after a short amount of time she suggested that he stop, for he looked like a man standing in front of a mirror practising poses.
She suggested that he stand in the lounge room while she asked him questions. After about five minutes, she suggested that he should stop because he looked like a right git.

"When you were the union rep at the factory, how did you ever convince anyone of anything?"
"Usually, I knew my stuff, what we were asking for, like numbers of hours or pay rates; what we could likely expect the bosses to say and maybe what sort of threats we could make if we didn't get what we wanted."
"Threats?"
"Yeah, work to rule, choosing not to do overtime... stuff like that."
"Well how come you can't use that experience here?"
"I don't know what the public wants. I can't threaten them with anything and I'm pretty sure that they can't really fire me for three years."
"You just don't look very confident."

"I don't know what I'm doing, I don't really know what I want and my cat has run away."

Katherine stood up and clapped.
"Well said sir. You sound more like a politician every day."

Chapter 8.
"You do not need a title to be a leader. A leader is a dealer in hope."

Monday, 17th Mai, 1000.

Even Radio 1 was abuzz in the morning with the rumour that the Minister of Defence, Betina Karenova had sent messages to KDP Central House, requesting a leadership challenge. Whilst Robert had been at church on Sunday and then spent the afternoon in a funk, the rest of the nation had forgotten about his indecision and diverted their attention to this instead.

Although Anton Diakonos was only a caretaker Prime Minister until proper government could be formed, he still for the moment held all the functions and responsibilities of the job; that job could be challenged.

After the fall of communism, the old Commune Assembly splintered into several factions which congealed into the current parties. The Socialist Robots were the remnants of the old workers' collectives and the United Labour Party assumed what would have been trade unions, had they existed at the time.

The KDP was different.

The KDP formed out of the old Politburo and monied interests who had made a packet from buying up ex-state run industries. Thus, the KDP retained both authoritarian-statists, economic libertarians, as well as anarcho-capitalists.

Anton Diakonos who used to be a member of the old secret service, was one of the few members of the party whom the old guard respected; yet instilled fear into new members of the party.

The challenge which came from Betina Karenova was reasonably sound. She was one of the new monied members and her fortune had come from selling rare-earth metals to mainly German high-tech companies. She had hoped to gain enough support in the caucus room amidst the uncertainly of the lack of formal government; claiming that Anton could no longer control either the parliament or the members of his own party.

Print media could not cope with the rumours and had missed out entirely. They tried to remain relevant by updating their websites as soon as anything came to hand but it was Channel 5A and Channel 12 who managed to put cameras on the ground first. Apart from the occasional murmur from television sets, the halls and offices of The Shortcake remained deathly silent as no-one was prepared to say anything to anyone. Robert parked his car in the secure car park and went to his office but saw no-one as he walked through the building.

At nine o'clock, there was a quiet exodus to one of the rooms on the third floor and even as cameras rolled, the most that they could get out of any KDP member was a wave or a smile.

The country waited.

By half past ten, the country was still waiting and the doors to the room on the third floor remained closed. By now, camera crews from all the television stations had arrived and the usual microphone operators from the radio and print networks were also in place.

The country waited.

At a quarter to midday, the door had still not opened and the media crews began to look inept as they flailed and flapped about with no news to report.

At seven minutes past midday, Robert received a call from Sophia Drazic. She had left her inner door open and thought that she heard a noise coming from the inner corridor. It was neither a member of the KDP; nor was it anything particularly interesting - a member of the Robots had gone to the smallest room in the building

When the door to the room was finally opened, the members filed out one by one and continued to remain silent. Although Anton walked past the cameras, he said nothing. When Betina Karenova walked past the cameras she was smiling and waved but still said nothing.

When all of the KDP Senators and members of the Commune Assembly had all gone past, the last person who left the room closed the door behind them and addressed the waiting media.

"There has been an extraordinary meeting of the Konservat Demokratik Party this morning. A decision regarding the leadership of the party has been made and the result is as follows."

Flashes started going off from still cameras. A light hush fell over the impromptu crowd. The party officer continued.

"The members have decided that no change of party leadership is necessary at this time."
"What were the results?" came a question from the crowd.
"I have just told you. There is no change of leadership at this time."
"Can you give us some figures?"
"It is not party policy to publish the results of internal meetings. I can tell you that a vote was taken by secret ballot and the party has decided that there is to be no change of leadership at this time.
Thank you."

The party officer bowed politely and walked off down the corridor; with some of the chasing media crews in tow.

Monday, 17th Mai, 1000.
Robert returned from lunch to see two reporters standing by the outer door to his office. After their morning scoop had gone cold, they reverted to chasing their other unresolved story.

"Does the result today change your voting intentions?"
"If Ms Karenova had won the leadership challenge this morning, would that have been enough for you to finally announce who you are going to support to form government?"

Robert put the key into the door lock, opened the door but before he went inside he spoke.

"I am holding a meeting in the Astari Town Hall on Wednesday night. Notices for this have already been published in local newspapers and another notice will be published on Wednesday morning.

I'm sorry but I will not be making any announcement until at least Thursday morning; after I have heard what the people of my constituency think."

One of the reporters left to use their time more productively; the other followed Robert into his office.

"Can I help you?" asked Robert; clearly annoyed that this person still hadn't got the message.

"We've been looking through the footage of St Iames Dinamo matches and have seen you in the crowd at the home end of the ground."
"It's not a crime to watch football matches is it?"
"Well no... what I was wondering is... St Iames Dinamo are at the bottom of the Liga Suprema and seven points away from escaping relegation. If you were the manager for St Iames Dinamo, what would you change up to improve the league standing?"

This was strange, thought Robert. He'd quite forgotten that the media did other things than chase politicians like hounds after a fox.

"The problem this season has been a lack of solid defence. Maybe if we switched to five at the back, we might stop the goals from leaking in.
I'd move Tycho to centre-back and Vyvyan to stopper."
"Do you think that you need any more firepower up front?"
"It wouldn't matter who was up front if they're not being fed quality ball. You can't score if you're constantly chasing your tail and picking the ball out of your own net."
"Would you sack the manager?"
"No. I think he's done an okay job. Maybe if there was someone better, it might be worth considering."
"Does that also hold true for the parliament?"
"Ahah. I know what you're doing. I won't give you the answer to that question before Thursday. Not before Thursday. You're both bold and sly. I like it."
"Thank you."

The reporter left; leaving Robert pondering if they would stop at nothing to get their scoop.

Monday, 17th Mai, 1000.
The fallout from the leadership challenge in the KDP was swift. Anton Diakonos held a press conference in the afternoon and told the country that if he was returned as Prime Minister, that he would lead a unified party with one purpose and attempt to reform the party. His voice sounded like an angry father scolding an errant child; clearly the underlying message was that he was going to undertake some sort of disciplinary action. Betina Karenova held her own press conference and said that she was threatening quit the party but when pressed she point blank refused to support Labour and the Robots; claiming that she'd rather quit the parliament altogether. If this was true, that would force a by-election in her electorate and that would stall the formation of government for an even longer period of time. By the end of the day, when things had gone off the boil and the heat had died down, nothing more was said by either Anton or Betina on the issue. This didn't stop the newspapers from publishing their guesses and theories in their evening editions.

As Robert drove home, radio commentary was picking this apart; wondering what this meant for the state of democracy if anything. If the KDP was eventually returned to power and Betina Karenova was installed as Prime Minister, did this represent a covenant of bad faith with the electorate? Considering that there was no position of the Prime Minister in the constitution anyway and all anyone ever did was vote for their local member, did this mean that the electorate itself suffered from cognitive dissonance?

When Robert got home, Katherine banned him from watching Channel 5A. Her tolerance and willingness to watch political discourse on television had already reached her recommend daily allowance and so they watched a movie on Channel 12 about a couple taking a trip through Africa. Somehow the sight of lions and hyena ripping apart a zebra was less brutal than watching people in suits tear metaphorical strips off each other.

Tuesday, 18th Mai, 1000.

By the time that Robert had driven down the M3 to the office the next morning, Ms Karenova had calmed down a bit. Clearly her position even as temporary Minister of Defence was seen by KDP Central House as untenable and she was officially demoted. Anton Diakonos hastily tried to quell the fires of speculation by telling a waiting media that no new minister would be appointed until formal government was formed but that didn't stop talkback radio from making all sorts of guesses as to who her replacement might be.

Robert pondered the idea that with this sort of vacancy, it would require a cabinet reshuffle and thus, if he were to throw his hat into the KDP ring, it might be worth considerable negotiating capital. After leaving the secure car park, he chose to walk across the public gallery rather than through the secure areas because he thought that being seen by the media and ending up on television, might persuade the whips and keepers at the KDP to give him something worth bargaining for but there were no cameras and no members of the press to be found at all. When he tried to phone up any KDP member, the lines either fell dead or were picked up by a secretary or personal assistant who explained that they were unavailable. Maybe there were disciplinary issues which the whips were trying to sort out. Whatever the reason for their collective silence, they remained unhelpful.

Tuesday, 18th Mai, 1000.

At lunch time, Robert left The Shortcake and walked towards Vayav's gas lamp district. The district was primarily made up of 870s era buildings and was something of a touristy area. Mostly the shops were selling tat to people who were easily amused. Long before Vayav had been chosen as the national capital, the old town was the centre of the then thriving coal industry. With the coal long since mined out and depleted, the town had gone into a sharp declined before the communists decided to move the capital here from Prihaaz in the south.

This area was called the gas lamp district because more than a century ago, this was the first city to be publicly lit with street lamps. The lamps which had all been converted to electric power years ago, now gave forth the jaundiced light of sodium bulbs instead of the bluish hues of gas. During the day though, the lampposts were like suspended iron birdcages, set against an azure sky.

Mirev & Hatsui's bookstore stood on the corner of 2nd Avenue and 3rd Street; in a brownstone building which miraculously had survived the ravages of war and civil disorder. The same could not be said for the inside of the building.
It wasn't that the old interior of the building hadn't survived, for it had done so most nobly; even down to the creaky wooden staircases that ran through the building. A bookstore is about the selling of books, literature and ideas, and the concept of book store had succumbed to the wars of trade of the late tenth century, soon to be the eleventh.
When the communists ruled the country, they also ruled the book shelves of the land. Book stores would carry great pieces of classic literature but modern classics which hinted at the capitalist system in the so-called free world, were banned. When the monarchy was restored, books no longer needed to be banned on the basis of what content they might contain, for the populace had simply lost interest in reading as once they did. Competition and erosion of sales forced the closure of many bookstores and the fact that Mirev & Hatsui's had survived was something of a minor miracle.

Robert, who was dressed in a blue shirt and black tie, was tapped on the shoulder whilst looking at a series of electric circuitry designer's manuals and was worried that someone thought he might work there. The person who had tapped him on the shoulder was a short fat man, slightly balding; with a long white flowing beard; who spoke with a voice from an old radio play.

"Hello son. Your name is Robert Ilanyich, I believe?"
"Yes, that's right."
"Come. We shall drink and speak of many things."

They walked down a set of stairs and to a small cafe inside the book store. The smell of coffee filled the air but Stanislav ordered 60 grammes of Vopob for each of them.

Vopob was said to have originated in Soviet occupied Germany in the weeks immediately after the close of the Second World War. Taking its name from its three components, vopob was made from vokda, port wine and blackcurrant juice; usually either Vimto or Ribena, which the British Army had in supply. Somehow this strange concoction had found its way out of adversity and into Plotchka in the 950s.

Robert looked into the small fluted glass in front of him. The liquid was purple and oily. He looked up at Stanislav. He wished that vopob had remained stuck in adversity.

"This is made in my home town of Rubiko. Vopob is hard to drink. It is like drinking the ink from a Biro. This is why it is so good. Many people drink themselves to death by vodka but because vopob is so vile, no one ever drinks themselves to death on vopob."

Robert sipped it. It was vile. He looked back at Stanislav.

"Why drink this if it is so horrible?"
"We do not drink to get drunk, for that is a silly idea. We drink because it is cold outside. We warm our hearts and we speak words of work and peace to each other."

Robert thought that Stanislav was as mad as a badger in a box of bananas but said nothing. Stanislav saw the look on his face and read it instantly.

"I can see by the look on your face that you think I am quite mad; I think you are right.

I have voted with the KDP; I have voted against the KDP. I have voted with the Robots; I have voted against the Robots. I have voted with Labour; I have voted against Labour. All of them have accused me of being Satan at one time; all of them have praised me for being Santa at other times; all of them have ignored me for being Stan at still other times.

I am not under the sting of party whips; I do not feel any sense of loyalty to anyone within the Senate. I am Stanislav Karpaty, Senator of Skolwelt. The only sense of loyalty I feel is to the people of Skolwelt. They elected me, they expect me to speak words of work and peace into the Senate.

You are not Stanislav Karpaty. You are Robert Ilanyich. You are from Astari. It doesn't matter who you end up choosing to run this country for the next three years, the people who decide your fate then, will ask 'did you speak words of work and peace on our behalf?'

I have been a Senator for fifteen years and might continue to go on for the next three depending on what the people have said. If you want to continue in the job for fifteen years, then can I tell you to do just one thing? Listen to the people."

Robert paused to consider what Stanislav had said. He still thought that the man in front of him was as daft as a brush; even if he did look like Santa. Maybe he chose to look like Santa because he was as daft as a brush.

"What would you do if you were in my situation?"
"What would I do? The question looks vexing but it is not really. I would demand the top job and then demand to form a unity government. I have been in this place to see the very worst in people. One side does not temper the other. In parliament there are a hundred Satans for every one Santa. Demand what you can but remember before everything else to listen to the people."

Robert thought that this was sound advice, even if it did come from someone who looked like Santa Claus. He did wonder though, what was this man doing in the technical section of a book store? What had caused Stanislav to bump into him at all?

"If you don't mind me asking, what were you doing in this book store today?"
"Oh I can see that."
"Good. I don't doubt your powers of observation. You might not believe me when I tell you this though. The reason that I was in the book store was to find a good book dealing with sewing machine repair. You see, in a past life many years ago, I used to work in a tailors' shop."
"Ah."

"Being in politics is a game in which there is no end and the writing and debating on legislation wearies the body. You need to get out of those offices with no windows occasionally and you need to do something entirely different. I mainly make suits and clothes but lately I have been making Velveteen Rabbits for my grandchildren."

"That's pretty nice."

"There are some people in the world from which I enjoy being praised for being Santa."

Robert laughed.

"My boy, you also have the chance to play at being Santa. When you decide who to support, you will give the gift of power to one side and take it away from the other. You will simultaneously be Santa and Satan to various people; maybe even both to the same person."

"I still don't know what I should do."

"There is no 'should'. Nobody has the ordained right to rule a people; not even the king. Politicians only rule with the consent of the people. Maybe that's the best way to answer this. Who do you consent to rule over you? Moreover, I know that you can't have put any of the others as number one on your ballot paper, so who did you put down as two, three and four?"

"I…"

"Don't tell me. They call it a 'secret ballot' for a good reason."

Tuesday, 18th Mai, 1000.

By the time Robert returned to the office from lunch, there were a heap of messages which had backed up on his voice mail. There were a few from Yeshua Guldblat, the Mayor of Astari; who was already working like a steamship chasing the blue ribbon, on making sure that the meeting at the Town Hall the next night, went off without a hitch. There was one message from Anton Diakonos who had requested a meeting with Robert at two o'clock but one immediately after it which cancelled that request again. When Robert tried to phone him back, he reached Anton's secretary.

Lastly there was a message from Katherine, who wanted to know what time the Town Hall meeting was supposed to be. She wanted to make sure that she could finish work and meet him there but when Robert phoned her back he explained that it would begin at eight o'clock.

"I'll be home at the normal time; so I think I'll have my dinner like normal and then we'll go out together."
"Will you have enough time?"
"The Town Hall is not even five minutes away by car. I used to walk past it every day to get to the factory."
"Are you sure?"
"Our town is so small that if someone on the other side of town left their fridge door open, you could throw a packet of green beans from where you were standing and probably get it to land next to the tomatoes; from anywhere in town."
"Only if you're sure."

Chapter 9.
"You always admire what you really don't understand. We are drowning in information but starved for knowledge."

Wednesday, 19th Mai, 1000.
The whole entire of Wednesday was a day that Robert could do without. What was Wednesday for? Some people back at the factory had called Wednesday 'hump day' as though it were a thing to get over or a thing in the way which designed to slow you down. Wednesday was the sort of day which those people who lived for the weekend considered as nothing more than filler.
In short, Wednesday was pointless.

Robert arrived at his desk and saw only a single sorry piece of mail. He opened it up and it was an invitation to attend the 'hundred days' party which was gazetted for the ninth of Aout. That was curious. Meetings and events were never 'pencilled in' or 'slated' but 'gazetted'; people 'minuted' things; and down in the parliamentary library the Parliamentary Record, which was colloquially called the 'Shortcake Book' or just the 'Shortbook' meant that parliament itself was either Shortcaked or Shortbooked.

Having still never appeared in parliament and never having to answer questions in public before, Robert was scared of looking like a complete fool at the Town Hall that night.
He decided that the best way to practice, since there was no-one else in the room, would be to read through a copy of The Globe and answer any questions which he saw in print. Unfortunately, there were very few questions in the newspaper and apart from those questions which asked if you knew how to save millions on your home loan or why a particular burger chain's burgers tasted so good, it was like trying to play Monopoly with half of the property cards missing, having only one die and nobody to play against.

By the time that five o'clock had rolled around, Robert had spent the day becoming progressively more paranoid about the evening and in a weird state of secretly wishing that a member of the press would arrive; whilst wishing that they'd all leave him alone.

He read through the list of procedures for when parliament would finally open, so that he'd know what to do and he wrote down an opening speech for the meeting; which he immediately threw into the wastepaper basket.

Most of Wednesday was pretty pointless. Wednesday was nothing more than filler.

Wednesday, 19th Mai, 1000.

As Robert drove back down the M3 and home, he turned on the radio to find the loudest, nastiest and most objectionable talkback that he could find. He turned it up and had a go at arguing with the callers who came on the radio. Mostly they were older folk who hoped that the government would increase pensions, or parents who wanted the government to reduce the amount of tax that they had to pay through the use of rebates. Robert got sick of all of that and switched the radio off. By now he was really nervous and kept on worrying if the audience would like him or not.

When he did make it home, he didn't realise how tired he was. All he wanted to do was fall face first into the couch and hope that the world swallowed him up.

Katherine heard Robert close the door to their apartment but was in their study; watching a Dutch television show on the internet.

"What're you doing Robert? We have to go in less than an hour," called Katherine from afar.

"I know," replied Robert.

"You can have you dinner when we get back home if you like. We can reheat it."

"Thanks."

It felt as though time had dilated and that it was spinning very quickly indeed, even though it had been barely five minutes since he'd got home.

Columbine and Harlequin came and sat next to Robert on the couch and just the simple act of stroking two cats, was enough to set his mind at ease; so much so that by the time that Katherine's program had ended, she found Robert, Columbine and Harlequin, all asleep.

"Wake up sleepy head. I hope you're not that relaxed when you go on stage tonight."

Robert failed to see the funny side to that.

Wednesday, 19th Mai, 1000.
Anyone who has ever organised a meeting of ten people knows that you will end up with thirteen opinions. If you were to multiply that by a couple of hundred then the resulting number of opinions is both nebulous and strange; it defies the laws of mathematics and logic.
That was what Robert expected before he went on stage at the Town Hall and as he stood in the wings, it was all he could do to remain calm. Just before he trod the boards and ventured out beneath the proscenium arch, Katherine brushed his suit and adjusted his tie.

"You'll be fine. The people out there voted for you. They want to hear from you. You're the reason that they showed up tonight."
"To tell you the truth, I'm really scared."
"Fake it until you make it? I don't know. You're pretty good at talking rubbish with your friends; so why not talk rubbish with those people. They won't know if you get it wrong."
"You'll be fine."

Robert was not so sure.
The Mayor of Astari Yeshua Guldblat, as the master of ceremonies, was truly 'the master of ceremonies' in every sense of every word. He was the 'master' in that he directed proceedings like the conductor of a symphony orchestra or the ringmaster of a macabre circus. He certainly had a sense of 'ceremony', of pomp and of the theatre of it all. He was also 'the' master; no-one could hold a candle to his brilliance that night, as his wit and ability to command the centre stage shone into the night.
Robert did not.

Robert faced the crowd and expected to be roasted. He did not expect however, the cavalcade of sop stories, hard luck takes and disappointments which came his way, masquerading as questions.

As their new member of parliament in the Commune Assembly, he was charged with the responsibility of representing them in that parliament. They, at least that night, expected a messiah figure who would save them from themselves and perform miracles and magic; conjuring up everything they desired. Their questions fell like rain on a metal roof – noisy, numerous; mostly useless.

"Can you do something about the children's' section of our local library?"
"May we have a therapy pool at the swimming centre?"
"My backyard keeps on flooding after a long period of rainy weather. Can you do something about having the stormwater drains diverted?"
"My daughter was diagnosed with cystic fibrosis and requires constant care and attention. I had to quit my job so that I could look after her and my insurance company won't pay income protection insurance because they say that it isn't covered by the policy. Can you sue the insurance company on my behalf?"
"When is the government going to do something about the teenagers who keep on hanging around the bottom of our street?"

Katherine who sat in the third row, could only watch on as her husband answered question after question, in arears and topics which he was not responsible for. The crowd grew ever more impatient and irascible as he explained that he was largely powerless to do anything about most of their issues because they were matters for other people.
He had accidentally called down the punishment of being a politician on himself and although he was coping with the pressure, he had no-one but himself to blame for this. After all, he had organised the town hall meeting in the first place.

"Mister Ilanyich, I am a single mother with two children and live in a state housing apartment block. I work three jobs as a shop assistant, a cleaner and at night I work as a cook in a very expensive restaurant. The image that society has of people like me is that we must be lazy or must work harder if we want to get ahead but I'm already working three jobs; none of which have holiday or sick leave and none of which have any real job security or regular hours.

My question is 'will you work with the Robots and Labour to fight for better working conditions for people like me or will you back the KDP?'"

Robert thought carefully before answering.

"As yet, I haven't yet declared my support for anyone I can't speak for the policies of those people that I haven't negotiated with but I too used to work in a factory where overtime was nonexistent and where the factory owners regularly held back our wages. I know what it's like not knowing how that next bill is going to be paid; so I thank you for voicing your concerns."

A man in an orange trades' shirt was next. His shirt looked so crisp name clean, it was as though it had never even been near a worksite.

"Good evening. I run an electrical fitting business. We go into building sites after the builders and plumbers have been and connect all the electrical lines and power outlets up. When you plug your toaster, your radio, your hair drier or your microwave oven in the wall, people like me will have rigged it up before the house was finished.

I employ about two dozen people and I have to pay for things like payroll tax, liability insurance as well as company tax and licence fees.

When I run my business, I can't afford to borrow too much money because it has to be paid back. When I run my business, I look at the costs and try to make sure that we're within our budgets and stay on cost.

Mister Ilanyich, six years ago when Labour and the Robots were in power, they racked up debts which we're still paying off. What I want to know is, do you intend to make sure that the government lives within its means and will you support the KDP to cut waste and pay off the debt?"

"I think all of us understand why you should live within your means and so reducing government debt is always a good default idea. We also need to ask why we're going into debt and as a businessman you'd appreciate that sometimes you need to invest in new plant and equipment to grow the business; the government needs to look at that sort of thing to grow the economy.

I would work with either side if their ideas are sensible enough."

One question came from a lady in a black T-shirt with the logo of some heavy metal rock band on it.

"Who do you like better, Anton or Petr?"

Robert thought about his answer. He didn't really know anything about either of the two leaders and didn't think that this mattered.

" When I hire a plumber because the pipes in my apartment have broken, I don't really have to like them. When they've gone, I might not see them again for a very long time. I would hope that they do such a good job that I don't need to call them back out again for a very long time.

I don't know Anton or Petr and I suspect that apart from what we hear on the television and radio, most of us don't either. We expect that they'd do such a good job, that we don't really have to hear from them."

"Is that the same for you?"

"I would hope that you hope so. Part of the reason that I'm here is because I want to do a good job for you so that you don't need to complain about me."

The next question came from someone whom Robert suspected had been handpicked by the mayor to cause trouble. This man wore a slightly grubby yellow polo shirt and had the look in his eyes of someone who didn't think that common sense was that common. It was the look of someone who was frequently visited by Uncle Kirov.

"What're'ya ga'an do about dole bludgers?"

Some audible gasps came forth and apart from a brief moment of muttering, the Town Hall was deathly silent.

Robert scanned the crowd and knew that he would be mobbed and torn asunder by precisely one half of the crowd if he didn't answer according to their expectations. His was the one seat in the whole house which had not yet declared its allegiance. He felt like Schrödinger's Cat in the moments before anyone opened the box; still alive but soon to be dead and happy to be left alone.

The one face in the crowd which could have smiled at him, Katherine's, did not. Katherine looked pensive and worried as the question hung in the air. Damocles hadn't just sharpened his sword, he'd been to the swordsmith and ordered a larger one.

"Section sixty-two of the constitution says that the government shall have the power to make laws to 'provide for the general welfare of all citizens.' You might not think of it when you look at them but someone on twenty million Lek a year is part of the same country as a homeless person spending the night in Engels Park in Vayav.

We shouldn't think of people on the dole as bludgers if we don't know their circumstances. What is the difference between someone on twenty million and the homeless person? Hard times? A stock market crash? A family dispute? We don't know. We do know that someone on twenty million does not make it by themselves. They work for a company with many people under them. Are they also bludgers? Those who are rich would do well to remember that it is only a strong tree which allows the very top to grow so tall; those who are not would do well to remember that we are all in the same country.

What am I going to do about dole bludgers? Ask questions to see if the accusations are true or not."

The crowd was mainly satisfied with this and soon settled down into quiet boredom.

After the two fifty minute sessions, the meeting drew to a close and the crowd slowly filed out. They had asked sixty-two questions in all and only about a dozen of them bordered on the actual responsibility and power of federal government. Mostly they were provincial matters and local council issues. Some were private legal matters and one question which was a family issue, should have never left the walls of the person's house.

What had Robert learned?
Democracy itself was not broken. Democracy was alive and well and living in Astari. What was broken was people. People were mostly selfish. People could only see the world from their own point of view and their sixty-two questions showed that that's what most of them cared about. As their member of parliament, that was important because the cares of the people, should be what guides a member in representing them.
Communism had worked, or at least had continued to function for so long, by uniting the people against the common enemy of the state. Democracy, or rule by the people, would work if the people weren't selfish idiots. Actually, all systems of government eventually break down because most people in the end, are selfish idiots. Idiocy and selfishness eventually causes the machinery of whatever government system is in place, to rust, to decay and fail.
How as a local member of parliament were you supposed to represent that? Robert was more confused than ever.

As they went home, Robert was shaking too much to be able to drive; so Katherine sat in the driver's seat.

"Do you think I did okay?"
"You did okay."
"Do you think the people liked me?"
"The point of that wasn't to decide whether the people like you or not but to find out what they want. Did that help you to make your decision at all?"
"No."

Wednesday, 19th Mai, 1000.

With the hung parliament now racing though its third week, Robert remembered the words of Anwar Ul-Huq who had said that initially he would be offered nothing but might be given something as the situation became more desperate.

Robert had pretty well much reached the end of his rope. When he got home, he slumped on the couch and thought that he could distract himself with mindless television. He was wrong.

Suddenly there was a knock at the door. Having no idea who it might be at this time of night, Robert answered the door hesitantly.

Standing in front of him was their landlord Mrs. Zhukova who lived down on the first floor. In her arms was a very sleepy looking Columbine, who wasn't the slightest but apologetic for going missing. Mrs. Zhukova gave Columbine to Robert and he placed her on the couch where she remained. He tried to invite Mrs. Zhukova in for coffee but she declined.

"Oh thank you, thank you, thank you and thank you for finding my Columbine. We spent hours looking for her but never found here. Where was she?"

"Last week there was a kerfuffle when all those television people came in our building. Columbine ran down the stairs and because the door to the street was closed, she started scratching at my door. I called the council and they picked her up. They returned her to me this evening and told me that she belonged to you. When I came up here earlier, you were out; so she's been staying at mine for the evening."

"I can't thank you enough for finding her. If I can do anything, anything for you, please let me know."

"Oh that's fine. I don't need anything."

"Thanks again."

"Evening."

"Good evening."

Robert returned to the couch and Columbine lay next to him as though nothing had happened. Harlequin saw the Columbine had returned; licked her for a bit and then proceeded to ignore her and Robert in the flippant manner that only cats are capable of.

Channel 5A was in the middle of their nightly news program and took expert opinion from grey haired ladies and balding men, who had been around the game of politics so long, that they were assumed to know everything.

Channel 12 was playing "World's Worst Crashes Caught On Camera - 7"; Robert was sure that the only reason that this sort of show even existed was to fill up blocks of late night programming. Channel 8 was playing a crime drama which might have been interesting, had you not entered half way through, Channel 9 had a comedy from Germany which mainly involved a lot of word play that didn't quite translate well and Channel 5 was playing part four of six of a dramatization of Tolstoy's "Anna Karenina". Robert had read that in high school and had he been more diligent, he may have understood what was going on but sadly, one of the greats of Russian literature had passed him by.

Columbine lay on the couch next to him but fidgeted when he tried to stroke her. Harlequin sat staring out of the glass door leading to the balcony which was his favourite pastime. The cats were never allowed outside on the balcony, being six storeys up but they never really complained. It was only the sight of a bird on the balcony which caused any sort of fuss from them but for the rest of the time, they would stare at aeroplanes or clouds drifting past.

The cats were content with what they had and even they'd learned that if they wanted something, that they'd eventually get an answer. Why couldn't people be as accepting as that?

Katherine came and sat down on the couch next to Robert. She didn't say anything but knew that the best thing that one can do for someone in a funk, is simply to be there for them. Eventually, she decided to offer a small piece of counsel.

"Why don't you just ask each of the independents why they chose whoever they did? If you listen to their reasons, maybe your decision might become easier."

"That's a good idea. I think I might do that."

Robert went out on to the balcony and watched as the blinking lights from an aeroplane, passed silently; high above them. Whatever problems those people had, paled into insignificance in the view of the vast open spaces of the world. Robert mused that in a few months' time, his decision and this time too would pass silently into history; only to become an amusing footnote in a book of political history.

He would ask his fellow independents what they thought. It couldn't hurt, could it?

Thursday, 20th Mai, 1000.

The M3 was an uninspiring road; a river of grey bleakness that stretched into the horizon. The morning rain that fell, served only to add to an already depressing picture. This was a day on which even the charlatans who write horoscopes would tell their readership to stay at home because nothing good could come of leaving the house.

Radio 1 played songs by manufactured pop princesses with all the talent of a herd of feral cats but lovingly corrected with auto tune. Radio 2 wittered back and forth with inane and banal banter, specifically designed for the masses of half-asleep motorists who would rather have stayed beneath their blankets. Radio 3...? Nobody listened to Radio 3.

Robert drifted along like so many motorists, as though they were pollen caught in the breeze. His new car was up to the task which certainly made life easier but a new car still didn't change the fact that motorways are designed for people to get to places in a hurry; not to enjoy the drive.

Even the nation's capital had not woken up yet. Usually by about 8am there were signs of life but this morning most of the shops were still wearing their nightly hoardings.

When Robert did arrive at The Shortcake, the security detail was almost half excited to see anyone arrive. They of course did not express their excitement but Robert noticed that as they cleared his car to enter the secure car park, they were chirpier than usual. Even inside The Shortcake, it was abnormally quiet. The usual array of secretaries, ancillary staff and those members of the public wanting to take a tour of the building was mysteriously absent.

Robert opened his laptop and checked his emails, wrote to a high school who wanted to a make a class on a field trip in seven months' time, and went to the inner room to make a cup of coffee.

Today, he decided, he would speak to each of the other four independent members of parliament and ask them to explain why they chose to support their respective sides. Maybe if those reasons were convincing enough, he might finally make his own decision.

Thursday, 20th Mai, 1000.

Ivan Nilsson had originally made the call for everyone to vote as a block. Even within the four walls of that initial meeting there was angst and in the end, his wish dissolved. Unity of purpose would have been a worthwhile pursuit but Ivan could not even herd a tiny flock; the sheep had run in all directions.

Robert found Ivan in the inner office, typing away like a mad man. Ivan only used two fingers in what might be called a 'hunt and peck' technique but Ivan had truly made the style his own. Those keys once pressed, knew that they had been and they cowered, hoping not to be pressed again.

"Good morning Robert," said Ivan; suddenly self-conscious. "The wheels of government must be kept spinning, even if there is no business to be done."

Robert knew that he would have to come straight to the point. This was a man who was obviously very busy, very distracted and very uninterested in what he had to say.

"Can I ask you why you decided to run with the KDP?"

"I would have thought that it was obvious."

"I'm afraid that it isn't."

"As you may be aware, I represent the largest cattle community in the country. My constituents are very much affected by changes in commodity prices. Under the KDP, we usually have lower rates of income tax and company tax. I need to think about the needs of farmers, who unlike weedy little city boys like you, actually do real work to keep the economy going."

Robert took offence to this. The washing machines that the factory produced, which he had worked in only a fortnight ago, were shipped all over the world; thus bringing in vital export Lek.

"I used to work in a factory. I've worked in factories my whole life. I'm not some career politician like you seem to think I am," said Robert.

"You still have to eat," Ivan replied triumphantly.

Robert was dumbfounded. He couldn't find fault with what Ivan had to say because Ivan was doing his job, for his constituency, perfectly.

"If you wanted to see your business thrive, you'd have voted for the KDP too."

"If you like the KDP so much, why did you quit the party?" pressed Robert.

"The party and I didn't see eye to eye on issues like tariffs, quotas and protecting our primary industries. We used to have one national supermarket chain and now we have three. They constantly compete on prices; which means that the poor farmers who supply them, are in a constant race to the bottom. I've heard tales of farmers even in my own constituency, commit suicide because they can't get fair prices for their produce. The people at the supermarket don't care. All they want are lower prices. Do you honestly think that 95 Lek bread is sustainable?"

Robert thought that Ivan's views were self-contradictory but he didn't say anything. Ivan looked like he was the sort of person who in his younger days, might 'accidentally' roughhouse someone and then deny that it had happened. Ivan came from the south of the country and whether deserved or not, southerners had a reputation for being brash and rash.

When Robert left Ivan's office, he saw three other members, standing on one of the balconies below. One of them immediately quick stepped his way out of there; presumably to inform party whips and strategists of the meeting which had just occurred. The telephone and email might be very quick ways of sending messages but rumour and intrigue have their own unique way of propagating; possibly at speeds even faster than the speed of light.

Thursday, 20th Mai, 1000.
Sophia arrived in Robert's office and after closing the door behind her, removed her shoes and left them next to the door. Robert assumed that this must be her custom and didn't mention it.

He led her to the outer office and they sat either side of the office desk. Robert offered Sophia some tea but she declined politely. In the world of politics and meeting after meeting, there was only so much tea that one could drink in a day.

"This morning, I saw you leave Ivan's office," said Sophia, "I can only imagine that he's convinced you to support the KDP. I can tell you, I'm not about to do that. I would rather remain in the wilderness for three years than support a government which I hated."

"That's not why I wanted to have this meeting."

"It isn't? Why else would you have called me here? If it isn't to change my opinion, then I honestly can't think of any other reason why you'd want to speak to me."

"Well actually, I've still not made up my mind who I'm going to support. I want to hear your decisions for joining Labour and the Robots."

Sophia looked at Robert as though he was trying to deceive her. She did not believe that he was either that simple or that clueless. She had previously been a member of the KDP and even been a cabinet minister and knew full well that the game of politics was the dirtiest, most underhanded game yet devised. In more barbarous times, people would kill each other to get where they wanted to go and get what they wanted; the only difference between ancient barbarism and modern civility was that people wore nicer suits and didn't want to get them dirty.

"I'm telling you outright – I don't trust you. But seeing as I genuinely don't know what your motives are, I suppose that I should tell you why I chose the coalition.

Twelve years ago, the KDP government which I was a part of, decided to privatise the electricity, gas and telecommunications networks. I was against the privatisation of all of them because they were and still are immensely profitable and they returned strong dividends to consolidated revenue. By selling off government businesses, we've forgone those dividends and have to make up the difference through either higher taxation or borrowing more.

I remember having a meeting with the finance minister over this very issue and he said that it wasn't appropriate for the government to compete with private enterprise. Ha! What he really meant to say was that he didn't think that it was right that normal people should get any benefits from profitable businesses. That particular minister has now left the parliament and now sits on the boards of both Plotchka Telekoms and Plotchka Dinamo, earning one point two billion Lek a year. Not million but billion."

Robert was horrified; he couldn't even conceal the look upon his face. How was this sort of thing even allowed?

"Wow. That's definitely given me something to think about."
"Well it should. Labour are ambivalent about it but the Robots want to see everything resumed and re-nationalised. They might be completely bonkers when it comes to turning businesses over to the workers but at least they're willing to negotiate on things"
"I'll keep that in mind."

Sophie looked at Robert in a confused kind of manner. Maybe he genuinely hadn't decided who he was going to support. Robert's office phone rang and he apologised for the interruption; saying that he needed to take the call. Sophie understood and walked to the inner door but made a deliberate show of leaving via the outer door; hoping that members of the press would interview her but they were nowhere to be found.

The call which had interrupted the meeting, was from Marie Androva. It was a voice which could have only come from Eoss Plotchka, just like his own, but apart from this, he knew very little about this former solicitor.

Thursday, 20th Mai, 1000.

Marie invited Robert to her office, knowing that he would be seen by someone on the journey over there. When Robert arrived at her office, he was greeted by her secretary, who could have only been paid out of her private funds, since unless one was a cabinet minister or in a position of power within one of the major parties, there was no allowance for the salary of a secretary.

Marie's office was practically identical to Robert's; right down to the position of the power points on the walls. With just the addition of just one person though, the office felt claustrophobic. On her desk was a stack of papers about three inches thick; along with the agreement which she had signed with the KDP. Her secretary was thumbing through the papers, apparently looking for something but seeing as they'd only been in the job for less than three weeks, it wasn't immediately obvious what they were looking for; nor why there would even be stack of papers on the desk.

Robert was impressed by the ostensible professionalism of the operation. If there was anyone suited to be a new member of parliament, it was Marie Androva. He felt slightly embarrassed to even be there.

Marie had called Robert to her office specifically because she wanted everything minuted. Her time spent in the legal profession meant that she was disciplined and efficient in managing her affairs. She also gave off the impression that she knew exactly what she was talking about and could name any minute detail about anything within her power, instantly. She was therefore quite disoriented by Robert's question.

"If you don't mind me asking, what was it specifically what led you to choose the KDP as the best choice for the next government?"

Was he insane? Was he stupid? The question in her mind didn't even bear questioning.
"What do you mean?"
"I still haven't decided one way or the other as to whom I should choose to support in the next term of parliament. I thought that I'd better ask each of the four independents for their reasons and see if that might help me make up my mind."

"How can you arrive in parliament without thinking through the consequences of you're being here?"

"I didn't expect to be here."

"Surely you must have thought it was a possibility. It is very irresponsible of you as a member of parliament not to have thought through these eventualities beforehand."

"To tell you the truth, I'd only expected to win enough votes to claim back the expenses allowance. I never expected to win my seat; much less to be one of the few to hold the balance of power."

Marie's incredulity was quickly turning to scorn. She had worked hard at her profession for many years; building up a reputation and thought it both a reward and a privilege to serve her community and have a chance to make it a better place but this man was an upstart who just blew in on the wind.

"What is holding you back from your decision? Why can't you just decide for yourself?"

This was a question that Robert did not want to hear and did not particularly want to answer. He felt, like so many people, that the political process had abandoned the people and seemed to be serving its own interests.

"I don't particularly like either side. I'm now in the position where I have to choose from one of two blocks which over the last decade or so, have sold off the family silverware. That's why I'm finding it difficult to choose sides."

Marie thought about Robert's complaint; she thought it sounded puerile.

"One of the election promises of the KDP was to lower income tax and company tax rates. That can only be good for business. If businesses feel like they're better off, than they're more likely to employ more people."

"Is that true though?"

"Of course it's true. Everyone knows that it's true. The only people who don't think it's true are the Socialist Robots and their whole party is loony."

Robert decided to change topic. He felt like she was mocking him, though he wasn't exactly sure how.

"What made you choose to run as an independent, rather than for the KDP?"
"Oh that was an easy choice. The KDP and I have many disagreements when it comes to a whole slew of social issues. The KDP would like the state to decide on these things and I think that the state should stay out of as many issues as it possibly can. The smaller the state, the freer the people."

Robert wasn't necessarily sure if he agreed with that either but he decided to remain as respectful as he possibly could and took his leave.

He left via the outer door to the office and seeing that it was almost lunchtime, he decided to take a walk though Bolshinstivo Park, which had many empty plinths throughout – the majority of the statues torn down following the restoration of the monarchy.

It was whilst walking through the park that he was spotted by someone from Channel 12, who then attempted to interview him. As he tried to leave, he was joined by camera operators from both Channel 8 and Channel 5A, which caused a fair amount of commotion and by the time he had made it back to The Shortcake, the crowd of cameras and microphone operators from the press and radio was so large that he had to be escorted by armed security guards through a cordoned off section of the building.

He wondered if it was Marie who had tipped them off because she was the last person he had spoken to, or whether it was someone else. She definitely gave him the impression that if she didn't like someone or something, she might resort to any means necessary to exact her revenge.

Robert thought that his fourth and final meeting with David Zoran should be held far away from the prying eyes of the media; so he arranged it to be held in the parliamentary cafeteria; in the very bottom of The Shortcake.

Thursday, 20th Mai, 1000.
The problem with coffee is that it never tastes as good as it smells. That whiff as it dances in the morning air, is soon replaced by that dreaded notion that you've just paid 350 Lek for brown coloured hot water in a cup. Those franchise coffee houses try to console you by adding syrups with more E numbers than a packet of sour candies but in the end, does anyone really think that caramel popcorn or pumpkin spice is anything remotely like coffee?
The best cups of coffee are either had whilst standing up in the streets of Paris whilst waiting in line for a baguette or possibly in Milan, where twenty moka pots are kept on constant turnover. This was nothing like that.
The coffee which David and Robert had sitting in front of them, was one step improved from instant and the sandwiches which they each had, were the last ones left, before the cafeteria closed.

David Zoran was the most weary of the five independents elected to this term of parliament. David had served on local councils for a very long time and experienced first-hand, that politics although often cited as the art of achieving the possible, was more often than not, the art of achieving the existing. There were plenty of people who had entered the game of politics with grand ideals, only to discover that the people with the biggest egos often bent people to their will; thus snapping their fragile little glass vials of ideals. David knew that Robert had never been in politics before and was not a member of a political party. This could either mean that Robert either had a forceful personality or had built up a reputation within his community. Robert's line of questioning was almost preternatural.

"What eventually made you choose to support the coalition?"
"Oh, not much really. They offered me a position in the cabinet but I didn't really like that idea – too much responsibility – but I did manage to convince the shadow roads minister that if elected, that the main town of the electorate which I represent, get an extension to a spur off of the M52."
"That was it?"

"Yeah, that was it. Look, I come from an electorate which apart from when they voted for me, had always had either Progressive Labour or United Labour representatives to the Commune Assembly. The KDP guy got less than ten percent of the vote; which meant that the race was between me and the Labour guy. I think that supporting the coalition is what my electorate wanted."

"What should I do?"

"What was the election race like?"

"Roughly a third each. I only won on preferences."

"How about your last few members?"

"We've had members from both Labour and the KDP."

"Then I'm afraid as though it sounds like you're caught in a very hard place to be. You should do what you think is best for your electorate, they're the ones who voted for you and then you need to think about what's best for the nation."

Robert was afraid of this. None of the four independents had truly left him with very much of a reason to tilt either way. They had all had their reasons for going the way that they had and they all had their own personalities, which also influenced how they voted but none of this was all that helpful in guiding him. He was still faced with the biggest decision of the parliament and pretty well much had to make it on his own.

Friday, 21st Mai, 1000.

Everyone says that they like Fridays. What they actually mean is they like going home at the end of the week. Friday mornings are mostly like every other day of the week and virtually everyone hides this fact so far deep within their soul that they're practically walking on top of it.

Robert hated Fridays and always had done for as long as he could remember. Fridays always held out the promise of being a good day but never ever were. Friday wrote cheques that it could never cash. Friday was a nasty piece of work.

The promise Office of Parliament demanded that every Friday, Members of Parliament; both from the Commune Assembly and the Senate, fill in their time sheets and their expenses claim forms.

Friday in this job was like any other job that Robert held, in that he was still being asked to clock on and clock off as though he were a cog in a giant machine. Still, if they were throwing more than three times his previous salary at him, maybe being a cog wasn't such a bad thing to be after all.

At about ten in the morning, he heard a commotion coming from down the hallway and poked his head out into the outer corridor. At least a dozen MPs were all heading in the same direction and so Robert thought it worthwhile to follow the crowd.

They all entered the Great Hall of Vlad which sat between the two chambers of The Shortcake but when Robert arrived at the entrance doors, he found out that this was an United Labour Party meeting and he was refused entry. He went back to his office.

Parliament was about clubs within clubs within clubs. He was reminded of the Ezekielian panjandrum with its wheels within wheels and wondered if it too was designed by a caucus meeting of some sort. The eternal triumvirate probably didn't need to seek cabinet or caucus approval before it built anything though.

Friday, 21st Mai, 1000.
In a particularly quiet moment later that morning, Robert's phone rang. Telephones were prone to do that but this mass made more noticeable because of the way that it rudely pierced the silence. The voice at the other end was unknown and the announced themselves as Kiel Dienstag, which was a name that Robert had never heard of before. Kiel was a Senator from his home province of Eoss Plotchka and had a voice cut raw by years of tobacco use; even the Minister for Industry would have thought that he was a walking offender of the Industrial Clean Air Act 981.

Kiel asked Robert to meet him the Royal Rose Garden, which nestled in between two of the spokes of the great wheel of the city.

Despite years of smoking like a coal fired power station, Kiel had the skin of fine porcelain. Robert was worried that if he sneezed, he might chip the glaze. Kiel was a short round object, like the sort of thing one might use to preserve fruits in.

Kiel was already part way through a cigarette when he saw
Robert coming towards him. He barely acknowledged Robert's
presence.

"Mister Dienstag, I presume," said Robert; reminding himself
one famous meeting in Africa.
"Morning, Robert," wheezed Kiel.
"You asked me to meet you?"
"Yes. I'm here to warn you about a few things; while you're still
a new boy and full of unnecessary optimism."

This did not sound welcoming and Robert remained on guard.
Kiel continued.
"This place eats fellows like you for breakfast. The reason why
most of the people even get to be in here is because they're all
scoundrels and rouges; the sort who would sell their
grandmother's kidneys if it meant a few Lek."

Robert was apprehensive. Was Kiel telling him this by way of
warning? That porcelain face revealed nothing; remaining static.

"Don't think you can trust me either. I've knifed people in the
back over the years, let me tell you. No, I'm not here to help you.
I'm here to tell you exactly where you stand, just in case you still
have any doubts left.
Your place is deadlocked and it doesn't matter which way you
fall, the margin on the floor will still be nil because whoever
does form government will lose one member as the speaker of
the assembly. My place is controlled by us but only for the
moment. At the end of the month, Labour loses two seats, the
KDP loses three and the Robots lose six. Those eleven seats will
be filled by fruits, nuts, vegetables who are beyond their sell by
date and two meat axes from a neo-fascist right wing party.
Whoever does finally form government is going to have to deal
with all of that."

Kiel returned to his cigarette. This was why the meeting was
being held out here. Robert was afraid to ask Kiel for advice
about his decision and so he changed the subject.

"Do you have any advice for someone just starting out?"
"Just two things.

One: always try to remember everyone's names. It is the mark of insincerity to be speaking with someone and not remember their name.

And two: always remember everything that can be used to attack someone in future. If you find any piece of scandal however small, do not tell anyone. That small thing can be used to blackmail and influence people later. Hold it above their head if you can, so that they don't know what you've got. In this game, almost everyone has some unsavoury thing in their past."

"Thank you, I guess."

"Kid, if you do decide to choose the KDP I'll see to it that you're given a nice cushy job, with not much hassle. I'll chat to the whips and party leaders. If you decide to go with that other lot, I will personally see to it that your days in this place are as unpleasant as they can possibly be. You won't even be able to walk down the corridors without trouble.

Chapter 10.
"Good resolutions are like babies crying in church, they should be carried out immediately."

Thursday, 20th Mai, 1000.
The mail arrived as it always did and apart from the usual stream of requests to appear at the opening of things, or a public speaking engagement, there was now the odd letter which contained nothing but abuse. People were beginning to get angry that no government had been formed yet, even though the administrative functions of government were still being carried out like they always had done. The public service was still serving.

There was a knock at the inner door. By now Robert was used to other members arriving to question him about who he would support, or others trying to convince him to throw his hat into their ring. Both sides had dug in and the party whips didn't particularly mind because they knew that sending in the privates was safe. The only patch of ground left to conquer was the barren patch in the middle, which when taken, ensure final victory.

The person that Robert met at the door was unknown to him, which in itself was not unusual in a parliament of one hundred and twenty five; the thing that really was unusual was his first words.

"I am a Robot."

That phrase in any other circumstance would be amusing but in this doorway, it was an uninteresting statement of fact.

It was Iago Romanov, Member for Orts; sitting member for nine years. He wore a tweed jacket with a square ended hessian tie ad a toothbrush moustache.

No-one ever dared ask him if his moustache was inspired by Charlie Chaplin or Adolf Hitler or if he wore it with the seriousness of one and the humour of the other or the humour of one and the seriousness of the other. He either wore his moustache ironically or unironically and his accent from the working class north, completed the picture so well that he remained both a question and unquestionable.

Iago was carrying a large, black, leather portfolio, with a gold Antifascist Circle embossed on it. The Robots had appropriated the logo as their own and the three arrows were said to represent the three enemies of social democracy as they saw it: monarchism, communism and capitalism. Did this mean that the Robots were actually opposed to themselves?

Robert was so taken aback by the appearance of this man that he led him to the inner room of his office almost immediately. He was kind of embarrassed to have him standing there.

"How can I help you? You said you name was?"

"Iago Romanov; call me Iago."

"I'm pleased to meet you Iago. Do take a seat. I'm Robert."

"Thank you."

"Now you can probably guess why I'm here. Like everyone else who has entered your office in the last few weeks, there is only one pressing matter on people's minds.

"Indeed."

"Let me assure you, I'm not here to ask you to join our party, even though our research indicates that you used to work in a factory and that would dovetail nicely into our ideology."

"Good."

"I'm here to make you an offer; an offer which I hope that you'll find acceptable and that will ensure that all of us can go on for the next three years."

"Go on."

"Let's be fair about this, it isn't worth your effort to support either bloc unless you are given a position of reasonable authority within in cabinet. We, that is the Socialist Robot Party, could easily solve the problem of government ourselves by switching our allegiance to the KDP but we find that we detest every single one of their domestic policies and most of their foreign policy and so that is as likely as deciding that you'd like to have a dead dog for dinner.

Our offer is this. If you support us, we'd make you Minister for Industry or Trade but we wouldn't expect you to join our party. You'd remain an independent and be free to vote against us on matters except for confidence and supply."

"Who would be Chief Exchequer or Prime Minister?"

"We would appoint Anwar Ul-Huq as the Chief Exchequer because he is the most qualified and capable of carrying out that role."

"And the Prime Minister?"

"That would naturally be myself."

"I didn't think that the Socialist Robots liked to appoint a leader."

"Correct."

"Then why would you appoint one? The position is not mentioned in the constitution."

"The people expect one. We believe that the power of the executive is held in the cabinet. The Prime Minister, if one should exist, really should only be the chairperson of that executive. If I am Prime Minister, I expect to be a very much hands off premier. Cabinet Ministers should be allowed to run their departments with minimal interference from a person, without portfolio; in charge of nothing."

"I see."

"We have taken the liberty to draw up a document, listing how this would all work. Please have a look at it."

Iago opened his portfolio and handed Robert a three page document on yellow paper, usually reserved for faxes. It had a list of prospective targets for various cabinet posts, including the two other aligned independents, David Zoran and Sophia Drazic. Robert looked down the list and noticed that Petr Brewin was notably absent.

Robert looked at Iago again. There was something more than a bit disconcerting about the man's face opposite him; yet there was nothing odd about him other than his moustache.

"What do you think about this? Are these terms acceptable to you?"

"Please give me some time to think about this."

"That is understandable. Please consider this carefully."

Iago shook Robert's hand and let himself out.

Was this the final answer? Was this how it was going to play out? Robert knew that eventually, he had to make his decision one way or the other and to be perfectly honest, there would not be any better offer from any other member. Was this really how the game of politics was played? On the floor of the chamber, the public saw shouting, the spitting of venom and bile and seventeen kinds of abuse being thrown but behind closed doors, there was just people behind desks, reading through reams of legislation and making mostly boring decisions.

Robert thought about the leadership challenge within the KDP and about how fractious that made the party appear. Even if he did throw his support behind the KDP, there wasn't the guarantee that the underlying issues which caused one member to threaten to quit the party, had gone away or even been dealt with. At least with United Labour and the Robots, theirs was an uneasy truce rather than an impending civil war. If Robert did support the KDP and members did cross the floor on a vote of no confidence, then the parliament would be brought into confusion again. He remembered the argument that he'd seen Petr Brewing having with someone on the telephone in the public gallery and wondered if the Robots had decided to inoculate their agreement by leaving him out.

Robert decided to wait twenty minutes before walking back to Iago's office. He would accept Iago's terms. The member of last seat in the house had finally made up his mind. In the end it wasn't what people were offering to him that finally swayed him but the hope of stable government; even though it was still possible that any agreements reached might collapse. At least with Labour and the Robots there was a more likely chance that the next election would be held in 1003 rather than later in the year.
Finally he was at peace.

He phoned Katherine. Katherine was both disappointed that Robert would not be the next Prime Minister but also happy for him. He asked her not to tell anyone because the press would be unrelenting in their questioning; that had already caused personal consequences. What the press didn't know, wouldn't hurt him.

He phoned Iago Romanov to inform him that his mind had finally been made up and Iago sounded as though he was paralysed with happiness. Robert would still not make the walk immediately but decided to spite one particular journalist by leaking his intent to both the New York Times and Joson Inmingun. The New York Times were happy to accept his phone call but no one in North Korea spoke Plotchkan; so Joson Inmingun would not get this scoop.

When he did make the walk to Iago's office, he looked around the building to see how many beady eyes were staring around doorways but he could see none. He knocked on Iago's door and Iago ushered him as quickly as he possibly could.
Waiting in the office was Petr Brewin, who looked dishevelled. Here was a man who had spent six weeks campaigning as hard as he could; with the expectation of gaining the premiership; only to see it all disappear in front of his eyes. He would remain on as head of the United Labour Party but it was a scant prize. Being head of the party but not holding a cabinet post, was both odd and humiliating.
Anwar Ul-Huq was sitting down with another gentleman over in the corner, drawing up the proposed calendar of events which had to take place before parliament could be opened.
The other two independents, Sophia Drazic and David Zoran were also waiting in the office. They were waiting to sign the Heads of Agreement document, which would finally being everything to a full stop; so that things could be started.

"So what happens at this point?" asked David.
"All the electorates were declared some time ago. At this point, someone needs to go and see The Doorkeeper of the Last Watch, who will invite the King to make the proclamation for the next parliament to assemble," explained Anwar.

Petr held his head in his hands. It was traditional for the Prime Minister-elect to accompany The Doorkeeper to the Winter Palace with the invitation but he now knew that this task would not be his. The Heads of Agreement excluded the United Labour Party from nominating one of its own as the Prime Minister and when the combined caucus would meet, the only name that would be put forward, would not be his own.
Anwar Ul-Huq spoke.

"I think that we should send Iago Romanov to accompany The Doorkeeper."

"I agree," said Petr, finally.

"I would like Robert Ilanyich to also accompany me," announced Iago.

"Why is that?"

"In a game of musical chairs, when there is only one seat left, when one shifts from left to right or from the right to the left, the art of the possible is achieved; today, that last seat in the house, achieved the possible."

Thursday, 20th Mai, 1000.

This ride in the back of the limousine was vastly different to the previous one he'd made nine days ago. This time he knew that he was supposed to be there and because he'd also previously met with the king behind closed doors, he knew that at the end of the journey was someone who was not his enemy.

The same ceremony with the presentation of the keys happened as it always did but unlike the last time he was here, it was not 'Jo' who met them but King Josep V in full military regalia.

Iago Romanov stepped forward and bowed; as did Robert from a distance. From inside his suit jacket, Iago produced a pre-written writ which if the king acquiesced to, would formally declare him as Prime Minister and request that the next session of parliament be opened.

King Josep accepted the writ, read through it, started clicking his tongue and wagged his head.

"Oh no no no. This will not do. This is not how we shall do this at all. Come."

King Joesp walked over to a writing bureau and sat down. He plucked a piece of shabby looking cream parchment from a small stack and began to write. After about three minutes in almost perfect silence, save for the soft ticking of a mantle clock, he finished writing and held the piece of parchment at arm's length; checking it over for spelling errors.

"This is how we shall do this. This writ will inform The Doorkeeper that I have appointed my representative to the executive. Tomorrow, when I open the parliament, The Doorkeeper will be the one who lets me into the parliament and it will be on his authorisation that I will even be allowed entry. The opening of parliament will proceed as per the constitution. Now then, as my representative to the executive, please sign here. This is where you give your consent."
"Thank you, Your Majesty."

Iago Romanov signed the document. He mentioned for Robert to come over and sign the document as well.

"This is why I called you to accompany me Robert. All legal documents require a signature and I preferred that you as an independent sign this, as opposed to someone from the ULP. Since this document will be kept on file forever, I wanted to make sure that nobody's signature from their party appeared here."

Robert understood exactly why he had been called now. Even on official documents, the alliance between the Robots and Labour was uneasy. He guessed that the only thing which really kept them together at all, was that a common danger unites even the bitterest enemies.

Friday, 21st Mai, 1000.
Katherine took the day off to see the official opening of parliament. It was something that she previously didn't care about and still wouldn't have cared about if her husband wasn't a member of parliament. She still thought that he was nowhere near qualified for the job but he had thrown himself into the role; he could throw himself out of it.
As the car rolled down the M3, Katherine realised that she hadn't been on most of the completed motorway yet. All of the little towns and hamlets which the highway used to pass through, were relegated to the status of just being words upon blue motorway signs. Those little towns and the businesses which once would have relied on the traffic passing through, would have all gone fiercely quiet and the roar of traffic was now out here, on two long ribbons of tarmac; stretching on from horizon to horizon.

Along one particular section, she glanced over at the speedometer and noticed that they were sitting on 190km/h. She looked at Robert who was already bored and immune to the thought but she was secretly terrified. At those sorts of speeds, one wheel wrong by anyone would put hundreds of people into the scenery.

On their left, an even quicker Italian sports car passed them and headed off into the distance, completely oblivious to the fact that it was travelling at more than four kilometres a minute. Even at the slower speed they were doing, they were still moving at fifty metres every second; that was still no consolation.

Katherine closed her eyes and tried to fall asleep. It was easier to shut the world out entirely than to try to deal with it. Clearly, the people who made trips like this every day had reconciled the fears with their need to get somewhere. With her eyes closed, it was like she was travelling without moving at all.

When they did reach the final climb into the mountains, Robert tapped Katherine on the shoulder so that she could watch the panorama of the city of Vayav open up in front of them. Katherine was unimpressed by this. It was a city, and not a particularly pretty one either. Even The Shortcake at the centre of six spokes of a giant wagon wheel, looked like a riotous mess. As the M3 dissolved into the A3 and became a wide boulevard with a median strip down the centre, Katherine tried to guess who the bronze statues which lined the road, were. She recognised no-one apart from Mendeleev and even then because he was holding a flask in on hand and a copy of his famous periodic table in the other.

When they did finally make it to the secure car park of The Shortcake and passed through the security section, Katherine was also disappointed that she would not be allowed on the floor of the Commune Assembly, even to look around after they were finished. She was not impressed. She would have to sit up in a gallery reserved for important people when the parliament was opened but at least this wasn't too bad.

Robert showed Katherine around the offices, the cafeteria and the 'Shame Room' before returning to his own office. Katherine was again not impressed, when she saw that there were no windows. With the doors closed it was like being on a submarine and equally as claustrophobic.

At a little after nine o'clock, someone arrived with the morning's mail and copies of the three bills which the United Labour Party wanted to introduce to parliament that afternoon. Even on opening day, there would be work to do in the house.
Of special note was a blue sheet of paper which indicated where people would be sitting in the Commune Assembly for the foreseeable future. Of course, this would be subject to change following a reshuffle but this at least was both an instruction as well as a handy guide.

"This is it, is it?"
"Yep. This is it."
"Are you scared?"
"A little bit, but this is far better than worrying about shape-changing lizard bosses back at the washing machine factory."

Katherine was finally satisfied. Instead of the prying eyes of factory bosses peering down on him, the nation would turn its slightly bored eyes upon him instead.
At five minutes to ten, a siren rang which Robert had never heard before. Katherine wondered if there was a fire in the building but as they opened the door, they saw a whole host of people in suits and jackets quietly walking, not towards the fire escape but towards the Commune Assembly.

"I think that that siren means that parliament is going to be opened. It must be like a five minute warning or something."
"I guess I'll see you later."

Robert kissed Katherine and she could only watch as he like one hundred and twenty-four other members walked out of sight. After asking an official in a very dapper blue uniform with gold trim, Katherine made her way upwards through the hallways of The Shortcake to a specially reserved gallery for dignitaries and other important people and she was quite pleased that she was not over in the crowded public galleries or the glass box reserved for the press.

From her position high above the chamber floor, she could see the whole of the Commune Assembly and could even see Robert sitting on the front bench along with the government. Along with the one-hundred and twenty-five members of the Commune Assembly were the sixty Senators. The building looked more crowded than it normally would do but it still was not cramped.

Somewhere down below, a trumpet blew a fanfare and everybody in the room simultaneously rose as King Josep was allowed entrance by The Doorkeeper of the Last Watch, Mikhail Kubasov.

The King took his spot at the front of the parliament, and after everyone in the room had exclaimed 'Long Live The King', he administered the oath of office to the Prime Minister and the various Cabinet Ministers.

At some stage during the last twenty-four hours, Marie Androva had also been convinced to lend her support to the Robots and Labour. The last seat in the house which had to be filled was the role of the speaker of the house, which a now humbled Petr Brewin accepted and his reluctance to ascend to the Speaker's Chair might have been genuine.

From high above the parliament; in the reserved gallery, Katherine's mobile phone beeped quietly. She pulled it out and read the message:

"The idea is stupid. I'll probably never be a politician either."

From one particular seat, the last one in the house to be decided, Robert waved at her.

END.